Race and Politics in the Dominican Republic

Race and Politics
in the
Dominican Republic

Ernesto Sagás

University Press of Florida

Gainesville · Tallahassee · Tampa · Boca Raton · Pensacola · Orlando · Miami · Jacksonville

05 04 03 02 01 00 6 5 4 3 2 1

Library of Congress Cataloging-in-Publication Data
Sagás, Ernesto.
Race and politics in the Dominican Republic / Ernesto Sagás.
p. cm.
Includes bibliographical references and index.
ISBN 0-8130-1763-7 (cloth: alk. paper)
1. Dominican Republic—Race relations. 2. Racism—Dominican
Republic. 3. Dominican Republic—History. 4. Dominican
Republic—Relations—Haiti. 5. Haiti—Relations—Dominican
Republic. I. Title.
F1941.A1 S34 2000
305.8'0097293—dc21 99-089361

The University Press of Florida is the scholarly publishing agency for
the State University System of Florida, comprising Florida A & M
University, Florida Atlantic University, Florida International
University, Florida State University, University of Central Florida,
University of Florida, University of North Florida, University of
South Florida, and University of West Florida.

University Press of Florida
15 Northwest 15th Street
Gainesville, FL 32611
http://www.upf.com

To the two peoples of Hispaniola

History is almost always written by the victors
and conquerors and gives their viewpoint.

Jawaharlal Nehru (1946)

CONTENTS

PREFACE

There is an intimate link between race, culture, and politics in the Caribbean, particularly in the former colonies of Spain. The elites of Cuba, Puerto Rico, and the Dominican Republic created racist, hegemonic ideologies to perpetuate their power and privileges. These racial ideologies have been accepted by or imposed on large segments of their populations. The case of *antihaitianismo* in the Dominican Republic is particularly poignant, as it has added an intra-island dimension to these Hispanophile dominant ideologies. Antihaitianismo ideology combines a legacy of racist Spanish colonial mentality, nineteenth-century racial theories, and twentieth-century cultural neoracism into a web of anti-Haitian attitudes, racial stereotypes, and historical distortions. Not only does this hegemonic ideology affect Haitian migrants in the Dominican Republic, but it has also traditionally been employed as an ideological weapon to subdue the black and mulatto Dominican lower classes and maintain their political quiescence.

This work is an examination and demystification of antihaitianismo ideology and its relationship to Dominican domestic politics. It unravels the centuries-old web of antihaitianismo ideology to show its common origins with other Hispanic Caribbean dominant ideologies, its historical development as a reflection of Dominican society, and its practical use as a political weapon, even recently. It utilizes an innovative, multidisciplinary theoretical approach (combining individual-level and sociohistorical interpretations) to explain the prevalence—and relative success—of antihaitianismo as a dominant ideology.

Antihaitianismo ideology has helped perpetuate an unequal class and racial structure that places Haitian immigrants at the bottom of the Dominican social pyramid, where they are unmercifully exploited. Moreover, antihaitianismo ideology has also served to keep the Dominican lower classes (mostly black and mulatto) in check, and to thwart any potential challenges to the hegemonic control of light-skinned elites. As such, antihaitianismo ideology certainly deserves to be studied not only for its impact on Dominican society but also for its linkages with similar dominant ideologies in the Hispanic Caribbean and elsewhere. The more we learn about how these racial/racist ideologies develop and operate, the better prepared we will be to confront and debunk them.

I still remember the day during my adolescence when a group of Haitian workers was not allowed to board the bus that I was riding in the Dominican Republic. Not one passenger stood up to defend their rights. The incident left me with conflicting thoughts and a bitter aftertaste in my mouth, and kindled my curiosity about Haiti. By the time I was attending graduate school at the University of Florida, this curiosity had developed into a research interest, and in 1993 I wrote my doctoral dissertation on antihaitianismo ideology. I have since presented parts of it at conferences and lectures, and it has been developed into this book thanks to the suggestions of friends and colleagues. An earlier version of chapters 3 and 4 was originally published as one piece in *Ethnicity, Race and Nationality in the Caribbean* (San Juan, P.R.: University of Puerto Rico, 1997).

Before thanking the many individuals and organizations listed below, I should tell the reader that though many of their suggestions were adopted—while others were not—the responsibility for the content of this work remains entirely mine. No single person was as important to the completion of this book as Orlando Inoa. Throughout many years, as fellow student, colleague, and friend, Orlando has deepened my understanding of Dominican society. His many suggestions, conversations, analyses, and amusing anecdotes have helped make this book a reality. Orlando and his wife, Lidia, were also my gracious hosts during my frequent visits to Santo Domingo, and they made my research trips enjoyable occasions. There is simply no way to repay them. I extend to them my heartfelt appreciation and a big *¡Muchas gracias!*

I visited several libraries during the course of my research, from the time it began as a dissertation project to the final completion of this book. I would like to thank the personnel at the following libraries and institutions for their help and cooperation: Archivo General de la Nación (Santo Domingo), Banco Central de la República Dominicana (Santo Domingo), Biblioteca Nacional de la República Dominicana (Santo Domingo), the City University of New York, Columbia University, Dirección General de Migración (Santo Domingo), Instituto Tecnológico de Santo Domingo, New York Public Library (Central Research Library and Schomburg Center), New York University, Pontificia Universidad Católica Madre y Maestra (Santo Domingo and Santiago), Universidad Autónoma de Santo Domingo, and University of Florida (Latin American Collection).

I would also like to thank some of my colleagues for their friendship and support. To a great extent, the completion of this book is the result of the expert guidance and mentoring of Forrest Colburn. Not only did Forrest read, reread, and edit the whole manuscript, but he also gave me all sorts of wise advice on sources, publishing, and even on the way the academic world operates. Forrest's editing, suggestions, and perspicacious questions made this book a much better work, while his advice and example made me a better scholar and human being. I will never forget his maxim: "Keep your eyes on the prize!"

Xavier Totti read a part of the manuscript and provided constructive comments. He also offered me his valuable friendship, which made Lehman College a great place to work in. By the same token, I must also thank Ceferino Carrasquillo, whose extensive administrative experience and warm friendship helped me navigate the waters of the academic world. The camaraderie of Jacqueline Jiménez-Polanco, Grisel Maduro, and Sintia Molina was something special that I could always count on, and for that, I am grateful to them. The help of Eugene "Gene" Laper, from the Inter-Library Loan office of the Lehman College library, also needs to be acknowledged. Gene provided me with much-needed books and articles, plus some very hard to find items, without which this book could not have been completed. My students were also an inspiring force in this work. Their comments and questions in and out of class, their thirst for knowledge, their disinterested help, and, in many cases, their friendship pushed me to perform to their exacting expectations. I would also like to thank the editors and staff at University Press of Florida for their help during the preparation of this book, particularly Meredith Morris-Babb, who was always a strong believer in this project. Finally, I thank my family for the time that this book took away from them, particularly my children, Antonio Ernesto and Anaís. To my parents, Eduardo and Nancy, goes my everlasting love.

Introduction

Race and Politics

At the beginning of the twentieth century, Francisco Moscoso Puello, a mulatto, described the Dominican people as "constitutionally white" (Moscoso Puello [1913, 1930–35] 1974; Baud 1996). Decades later, historian Manuel A. Peña Batlle described the Dominican nation as "Spanish, Christian, and Catholic" (1954b, 66).[1] While Moscoso Puello may have only been spoofing the desperation of many dark-skinned Dominicans to differentiate themselves from black Haitians, Peña Batlle served as the main ideologue of the nationalist dictator Rafael Trujillo. These assertions were made in different historical contexts, but both underline the seemingly permanent obsession of contemporary Dominican intellectuals with the issues of race—particularly in relation to Haiti—and national identity. Dominican elites, faced with the inescapable fact that their country shares the island of Hispaniola with Haiti, have erected barriers of prejudice and racism to distance themselves from their poor, dark-skinned neighbors. The same elites have also found race a useful political tool in thwarting challenges to their status.

A Racial Mirage

The Hispanic Caribbean is not usually considered an area plagued by racism. Visitors point to the apparent lack of overt racial prejudices in the racially mixed societies of the Hispanic Caribbean. Officially, the Dominican Republic is portrayed by its government as a tropical paradise, a racially harmonious society where whites and blacks have intermingled to give way to the mulatto (Casado 1998). This glorified view is only partially true. Certainly, as Harry Hoetink aptly explains, the perception of racial differences—what he calls the somatic norm image—is different in Hispanic Caribbean societies than in other parts of the Caribbean archipelago or the United States (1971, chaps. 4, 5). As a result of relaxed racial norms, blacks and mulattos have had a greater chance of upward mobility in the Hispanic Caribbean than in other multiracial societies. Indeed, the Dominican Republic has had several black and mulatto presidents. Official racial segregation has never taken place in the Dominican Republic during the republican period, nor has any racially based political movement ever been organized in the country.

But Hispanic Caribbean societies—and the Dominican Republic in particular—are not color-blind or free of racial prejudices. Racism has been an inseparable part of Hispanic Caribbean societies, in which race and social status seem to be intrinsically tied. Blacks and mulattos are still the objects of unofficial discrimination in Cuba, Puerto Rico, and the Dominican Republic, even though they make up a large percentage of their populations.[2] Even in Cuba, where a socialist revolution has actively encouraged the elimination of racial prejudice, blacks remain underrepresented in the higher echelons of government (Montaner 1983, 74–78). In all three societies, resources, power, and prestige are still largely in the hands of light-skinned elites.

The particular racial situation of the Dominican Republic thus resembles a mirage: there is apparent racial harmony, but with a strong underlying current of "unofficial" prejudice and racism. Moreover, much of this racism is directed toward its neighbor, Haiti (a nation where blacks make up 95 percent of the population), and the thousands of poor Haitians who have migrated to the Dominican Republic. As such, the Dominican case is a difficult one to explain using the current literature on race and prejudice. Most existing theories of racism are based on case studies of European nations (such as Nazi Germany), Africa (for example, South Africa's apartheid), or the United States (for example, segregation), and they cannot be applied to the situation in the Dominican Republic, where there are no discrete racial categories. Furthermore, the literature on ethnicity (Hutchinson and Smith 1996) and the management of ethnic (or communal) conflict (Esman 1973) also has its shortcomings, as prejudice in the Dominican Republic is directed not only toward Haiti and Haitian immigrants, but also—with various degrees of subtlety—toward dark-skinned Dominicans. This book attempts to enrich our understanding of race by studying a lesser-known case that falls outside the parameters of most studies on racism and prejudice. The emphasis here is on the ways in which elites can use race to construct national myths and then use these myths to stymie challenges to their hegemony.

National Myths

Elites in the Hispanic Caribbean (and throughout Latin America) have created nationalist-cultural myths to maintain their political supremacy and reproduce their racial views. These "color-blind" myths imply racial harmony in their racially mixed societies, while obviating black or Afro-Caribbean elements, and maintaining unofficial forms of racial prejudice toward the darker members of society. It is not surprising that the national folk figures of Cuba (the *guajiro*), Puerto Rico (the *jíbaro*), and the Dominican Republic (the *campesino cibaeño*) are depicted as light-skinned, Hispanic peasants—the supposed embodiments of the national soul. As regional icons projected into national myths, they do not, however, represent the different "realities" of their multiracial societies.

In the case of the Dominican Republic, which shares the small Caribbean island of Hispaniola with Haiti, these issues have taken on major proportions. Relations between these two countries have historically been tense and laden with misunderstandings, with only occasional instances of cooperation. Haitian armies invaded the Dominican Republic on several occasions in the nineteenth century, once even annexing its eastern neighbor for twenty-two years (1822–44). Dominican leaders have responded in kind by meddling in Haitian affairs and with the massacre of thousands of Haitian migrants in 1937.

In the Dominican Republic, this conflictive relationship has been manipulated to serve the racial views of the Dominican elites, and to serve as a powerful instrument to halt potential threats to their political and economic status. An anti-Haitian credo has emerged, which is a dominant ideology known as *antihaitianismo*. It can be defined as a set of socially reproduced anti-Haitian prejudices, myths, and stereotypes prevalent in the cultural makeup of the Dominican Republic. These are based on presumed racial, social, economic, and national-cultural differences between the two peoples; differences stressed by generations of Dominican ideologues. As a result, Haiti and things "Haitian" are scorned and rejected by Dominican society.

As an ideology, antihaitianismo treats Haitians as the scapegoats of a society that considers them racially and culturally inferior aliens who are barbaric and undesirable. But antihaitianismo is also an ideological method of political control. It is directed not only toward Haiti and Haitians, but also toward Afro-Caribbean members of Dominican society, who tend to be poor, forming the subordinate class. Antihaitianismo denies dark-skinned citizens, and the poor generally, their own sociocultural space and intimidates them from making demands or otherwise participating in politics. Thus antihaitianismo is a deliberate creation: it is an authoritarian, dominant ideology, with the objective of defending a narrow status quo.

Yet the persistence of antihaitianismo, and its success as a dominant ideology, cannot be simply explained by a "conspiracy theory." Antihaitianismo ideology has grown deep roots in the Dominican national psyche for reasons having as much to do with cultural and personal affinity with elite ideas as with power relationships. Antihaitianismo ideology, imposed from above, has also been somehow willingly accepted from below, where it has roots in national-cultural prejudices. Haiti, since its independence, has been the pariah nation of the Americas (Farmer 1994). As the product of a bloody slave insurrection and racial strife, the independence of Haiti in 1804 represented a terrifying prospect for white nations: the massacre of most whites, the destruction of European civilization, and their replacement by a black republic led by the ex-slaves themselves. Even the newly independent Latin American nations turned their backs on Haiti and excluded it from hemispheric deliberations, such as the 1826 Congress of Panama. In spite of its human achievements, in the minds of white elites the Haitian Revolution became synonymous with chaos, violence, and black savagery. If the Haitian Revolution provoked feelings of rejection by elites in the rest of the hemisphere, for the Dominican elites, neighboring Haiti was their gravest concern. Antihaitianismo ideology thus provided Dominicans with a convenient shield of cultural superiority vis-à-vis an ostracized nation. As contradictory as it may seem, and as a result of antihaitianismo ideology, even the lowest, poorest, and darkest Dominicans are prone to claim cultural—and even racial—superiority over the Haitian people.

Nationalism and Dominant Ideologies

No force in modern times has been as powerful as nationalism. Millions have been willing to kill—and die—for the abstract idea of the nation. Whether one calls it the Fatherland, Mother Russia, la France, or la Patria, the concept of the nation appeals to citizens by making them feel that they "belong" to a group apart. So influential has nationalism been that Benedict Anderson calls it "the most universally legitimate value in the political life of our time" (1991, 3). Nationalism, and the nationalist ideologies that it gives rise to, produce conceptions of peoplehood, that is, ideologies of common ("national") culture (Fox 1990, 3). These nationalist ideologies are cultural artifacts that imagine political communities; they invent nations (Anderson 1991, 6). It is widely believed that a shared culture and traditions theoretically establish the nation as a distinct unit. However, traditions have an ideological content, so the invention of the nation is selective: only certain items (like the *campesino cibaeño* or merengue music in the case of the Dominican Republic) are chosen to represent traditional national culture, while other aspects of the past are conveniently ignored or forgotten (like Dominican Afro-Caribbean culture).

Elites—in particular, historians—contribute to this process of "national engineering" by legitimizing traditions and shaping national culture. As described by Eric Hobsbawn, "All these rest on exercises in social engineering which are often deliberate and always innovative, if only because historical novelty implies innovation" (1994, 76). In the case of the Dominican Republic, this nationalism has typically been a response by the upper classes to popular vernacular nationalism (Anderson 1991, 150).

Elites have used the powerful force of nationalism in the construction of what essentially are dominant (or hegemonic) ideologies. The word *ideology* has been defined in many ways, but I use the definition presented by political sociologist Robert MacIver: "a system of political, economic, and social values and ideas from which objectives are derived. These objectives form the nucleus of a political program" (Bluhm 1974, 3). Thus, a dominant ideology can be defined as a system of values and beliefs that, by its ruling-class origins, overwhelms any other competing beliefs in society. Its main objectives are to "incorporate the subordinate classes, making them politically quiescent" and "to conceal social relations" (Abercrombie, Hill, and Turner 1980, 8, 29). According to Richard Fox, dominant ideologies can be so powerful that "the system of domination and inequality in a society becomes so culturally encoded, that is, lodged deep in cultural belief, that it comes to appear natural and inviolate" (1990, 12). As such, a dominant ideology is an important instrument of social control, mainly because "without ideological support, political power becomes 'naked power'" (Christenson and others 1981, 14). There can be other competing (or resisting) ideologies in society, but the dominant ideology, by the power of its elite origins, prevails.

Another aspect of dominant nationalist ideologies is their connection to prejudice and racism. Underlying the organization of nationalism as a political movement there inevitably is racism. According to Etienne Balibar and Immanuel Wallerstein: "All kinds of somatic or psychological features, both visible and invisible, may lend themselves to creating the fiction of a racial identity and therefore to representing natural and hereditary differences between social groups either within the same nation or outside its frontiers" (1991, 99). Thus elites not only invent the notion of a particular society based on a supposedly common culture and traditions, but also try to extend it to include a fictitious racial identity. In Latin America, this process took place in countries as disparate as Mexico, Cuba, Brazil, and Argentina.[3] In the Dominican Republic, antihaitianismo ideology created the myth of Haitians and Dominicans belonging to different races.

The link between nationalist dominant ideologies and racism demands a consideration of the origins and reproduction of prejudice. The causes of racial and ethnic prejudice range from general, sociohistorical interpretations to individual psychological explanations. The sociohistorical (or structural) approach looks for the causes of racism and prejudice at the national or supranational level. By examining a country's history, society, and culture, it tries to explain the prejudice of one group (or nation) toward another as based on deep-seated historical, political, or cultural differences. In contrast, individual explanations look at personal attitudes as the main cause of prejudice. Racism and prejudice, they claim, are individual acts caused by individual attitudes.

Caribbean Race Relations: A Study of Two Variants, the classic work of Harry Hoetink (1971) on the two variants of the somatic norm image in Caribbean societies, is an insightful example of the sociohistorical approach. Hoetink contrasts the Iberian somatic norm image that is prevalent in the Spanish-speaking Caribbean with the northwestern European somatic norm image of the rest of the islands. He concludes that there is a smaller somatic distance in the formerly Iberian colonies than in the other colonies. For example, a light mulatto is considered white (or whitelike) in countries within the Iberian somatic norm (Cuba, Puerto Rico, and the Dominican Republic), while that same person would be labeled black in countries within the northwestern European somatic norm (other Caribbean islands, the United States). That difference leads to a reduction—but not elimination—of racial prejudice in the former countries; it also encourages miscegenation.

Another illuminating example of the sociohistorical approach is *Raza e historia en Santo Domingo* by Hugo Tolentino Dipp (1992). This work analyzes the formation of racial prejudices in the first colony of the New World: Hispaniola or Santo Domingo. The main thesis of Tolentino Dipp's book is that the origins of racial prejudice had nothing to do with skin color. Rather, these prejudices had an economic basis: sugar production. The profitable production of sugar demanded a cheap and docile labor force (either Indians or African slaves), and racial prejudice helped justify and maintain this status quo that separated the white master from the black slave, the powerful from the powerless, and the wealthy from the destitute (Tolentino Dipp 1992, 223–24). Even more important, besides justifying this separation, racial prejudice provided an easily identifiable reference sign: skin color.

The study of racial tensions and prejudice is not limited to historical studies. Anthropologists, sociologists, and political scientists, both in the United States and Europe, have conducted valuable research on contemporary cases of racial and ethnic conflict. The work of Teun A. van Dijk (1987) stands out among these studied. In *Communicating Racism: Ethnic Prejudice in Thought and Talk,* van Dijk shows that prejudice is a group attitude and that these attitudes are "acquired, used, and transformed in social contexts" (1987, 195). More explicitly, he says, "Prejudice is not a personal, individual attitude toward ethnic minority groups, but socially acquired, shared, and enacted within the dominant in-group" (1987, 345). In this respect, van Dijk also follows the sociocultural approach, but from a different perspective. He interviewed individuals to assess whether their prejudices were mainly personal or social. He concluded that racism and prejudice are social phenomena that are learned and reproduced.

Van Dijk singles out elites[4] as providing the initial (pre)formulations of ethnic prejudices in society, and the media as their major channel for the reproduction of these ethnic attitudes (1987, 360–61). He says that "people do not spontaneously 'invent' negative opinions about ethnic minority groups, nor do they express and communicate them in everyday talk without sociocultural constraints. Prejudice and its reproduction in (verbal or other) interaction has specific social functions, which may simply be summarized as the maintenance of dominance or power for the in-group and its members" (1987, 359). For van Dijk, elites create (or maintain) most of these negative opinions with the aim of preserving their status quo, and they are in turn reproduced by the media—also controlled by elite groups (1987, 360). The general literature on socialization supports these claims and points to schools, parents, and the mass media as the main agents of socialization (Orum 1983, 266–72).

These arguments are also present in the literature on Haitian-Dominican relations by Lil Despradel (1974), who argues that it was the work of Dominican historians to keep alive and even create new versions of anti-haitianismo ideology, as well as to arouse nationalist feelings by exalting the "purely" Hispanic heritage of the Dominican people. The general public adopts these dominant elite opinions given "the absence or scarcity of alternative forms of discourse and information, antiracist models, and positive information" (van Dijk 1987, 363). In the case of the Dominican Republic, authoritarian power structures have reinforced these trends.

Van Dijk has also classified prejudice on the basis of three dimensions of "threat," that is, the supposed threat that foreigners or minorities represent to their host society. These threats are portrayed as economic, cultural, and/or social; foreigners or minorities represent an unfair economic competition, are culturally different and do not seem to adapt to the host society's cultural norms, and are social misfits who wreck the established social order (van Dijk 1987, 58–60). In simpler terms, they are "different" from the "established order," and that makes them the subject of prejudice.

Finally, van Dijk establishes five prejudice categories, based on elite (pre)formulations and their reproduction by the media: immigration, crime and aggression, unfair competition, cultural conflicts, and personal characteristics (1987, 364–66). Under these five categories, different prejudices are expressed that try both to denigrate (or dehumanize) immigrants and to portray them as a threat. (The majority of these prejudices have been applied toward Haitian migrants in the Dominican Republic.) Under immigration, van Dijk mentions the constant references to a "flood" of immigrants as one of the main prejudices found in the media (1987, 364). Under the crime and aggression category, he condemns the common media practice of specifying the ethnic background of crime suspects (1987, 364). In the unfair competition category, the main prejudice is the widespread belief that migrant workers "steal" jobs from native residents and burden socioeconomic resources; no thought is given to whether they are employed in activities that natives shun (such as farmwork and domestic work), or whether they contribute to the country's economic well-being (van Dijk 1987, 364–65). In the cultural conflicts category, most prejudices depict foreign cultures as "strange," "different," or "inferior" (van Dijk 1987, 365–66). Finally, in the personal characteristics category, immigrants are portrayed as stupid, lazy, uneducated, backward, and childish. These attributed characteristics then become, in the country's popular culture, the "typical" and everyday behavior of minority groups (van Dijk 1987, 366).

Individual-level explanations of racism and prejudice include Donald Kinder and David Sears's (1981) theoretical debate on racial threats versus symbolic racism. According to them, the racial threat hypothesis originates in the competition between blacks and whites in the United States for a share of the "good life" and leads to rational choice–type decisions (1981, 415). Whites discriminate against blacks to the extent that whites, as individuals, feel that their share of the "good life" is being threatened by this out-group. A similar argument is commonly made in the Dominican Republic about Haitian migrants, who are accused of "stealing" jobs and lowering wages.

The symbolic racism hypothesis stresses early life socialization processes, which influence adult attitudes and perceptions. Socialization results in affective responses to symbols, regardless of tangible consequences for the adult's personal life. For example, many white adults in the United States opposed busing black and white children together to integrated schools, even though they had no children that could be affected by that decision (Sears, Hensler, and Speer 1979). John McConahay and Joseph Hough probably present the best definition of symbolic racism: "It is the expression in terms of abstract ideological symbols and symbolic behaviors of the feeling that blacks are violating cherished values and making illegitimate demands for changes in the racial status quo" (1976, 38). Again, this argument can be made for the Dominican Republic, where Haitians are accused of "tainting" the racial makeup and Hispanic values of the Dominican people.

There is also an ample literature on ethnicity that has been used in the study of foreign or minority groups and their conflict with dominant groups. Donald Horowitz (1985, 41–54), for example, demystifies the presumed role of color in ethnic conflicts. Traditionally, color differences had been assumed to give rise to subordination and severe conflict. Horowitz shows that other features, or cues (such as physiognomy, hair color, gestures, dress, grooming, food habits, and accent), are as important as—and sometimes even more important than—color in establishing ethnic differences. Moreover, Horowitz corroborates that "ethnicity is based on a myth of collective ancestry, which usually carries with it traits believed to be innate" (1985, 52).

Milton Esman (1973) also examines the often-conflictive nature of ethnic relations. He defines communalism as "competitive group solidarities within the same political system based on ethnic, linguistic, racial, or religious identities," and identifies four classes of regime objectives: institutionalized dominance, induced assimilation, syncretic integration, and balanced pluralism (1973, 49, 56). The first strategy—institutionalized dominance—seems to approximate the case of the Dominican Republic, in which a dominant communal group subjects another to a permanent situation of inferiority.

The literature on authoritarianism may also provide clues to the political behavior of the Dominican elites. Juan Linz's classic definition of authoritarian regimes describes the use of distinctive mentalities, "which are ways of thinking and feeling, more emotional than rational, that provide non-codified ways of reacting to situations," and that are part of the dominant structure in an authoritarian system (1970, 257). Totalitarian systems, in contrast, employ ideologies "which are systems of thought more or less intellectually elaborated and organized, often in written form, by intellectuals, pseudo-intellectuals, or with their assistance" (Linz 1970, 257). Amos Perlmutter (1981) also examines the role of nationalist and racist ideologies in authoritarian regimes.

The main shortcoming of the literature on ethnic conflict for examining the Dominican case is that it has been mostly based on the experience of non-Latin American regions (that is, Africa, Asia, and eastern Europe). As Hoetink (1971) has shown, the case of the Caribbean—particularly the Hispanic Caribbean—is a very particular one, where discrete racial and ethnic categories are not present. Though interesting parallels with the Dominican case can be drawn from the work of Horowitz (1985), additional research is needed to substantiate his general assertions. The literature on authoritarianism suffers from even more serious shortcomings regarding its applicability to the case of the Dominican Republic. Most of its evidence is drawn from European cases (for example, Nazi Germany, the Soviet Union, Franco's Spain) or from the corporatist regimes of South America (countries whose political systems and levels of development are quite different from those of the Dominican Republic).

A more promising approach and partial redefinition of the Dominican case is the work of H. E. Chehabi and Juan Linz (1998) on sultanistic regimes. "[Sultanism] is based on personal rulership," write Chehabi and Linz, "but loyalty to the ruler is motivated not by his embodying or articulating an ideology, nor by a unique personal mission, nor by any charismatic qualities, but by a mixture of fear and rewards to his collaborators. The ruler exercises his power without restraint, at his own discretion and above all unencumbered by rules or by any commitment to an ideology or value system" (1998, 7). The essay by Jonathan Hartlyn in Chehabi and Linz's work (which just covers the period of the Trujillo dictatorship), however, mentions the use of anti-Haitian nationalism only in passing (1998b, 257–58 nn. 27–28).

Thus the literature on authoritarianism has slighted or ignored the role of race, and its manipulation by elites to maintain power, in several ways. First, it has not explored racial conflict in cases where racial identities are blurred, not discrete, as in the Hispanic Caribbean. How do you distinguish between a light-skinned mulatto and a "white," or between a dark-skinned mulatto and a black, when it is often difficult (and conflictive) even for those who fall within these categories to make the distinction themselves? Obviously, racial conflict is not very difficult to ascertain when the groups under study are racially different. In the case of the Dominican Republic and Haiti, it is precisely their racial closeness that exacerbates conflict, as Dominican elites have tried to forge a "white" identity to differentiate themselves from their "black" neighbors.

Second, though the literature has addressed cases of regimes fostering or controlling ethnic conflict, what about when a regime does both? In the case of the Dominican Republic, we may speak of regimes that simultaneously rejected racial conflict (the myth of national unity) while fomenting and camouflaging racism. The administrations of Rafael Trujillo and Joaquín Balaguer were two such regimes. While they proudly hailed their societies as "color-blind" and "prejudice-free," they also fostered a climate of intolerance toward Haitian immigrants. Thus they avoided the violence of open racial conflict but manipulated racism for political gain and the subordination of the lower classes.

Third, there has not been sufficient attention paid to the linkages between class and race. In the Dominican Republic, as in most of Latin America, there is a close correlation between class and race, with the upper classes being lighter skinned than the lower classes. In spite of that, most historical class analyses of Dominican society (for example, Marxist analyses of the 1960s and 1970s) have ignored or downplayed the race issue.

Fourth, although there is a generalized perception that ethnic and racial conflict is dysfunctional to a political regime, low-intensity racial conflict—by distracting public opinion and subjugating the poor—may actually be useful for a regime's survival. Dominican authoritarian and semiauthoritarian regimes, in their quest for legitimacy, have often resorted to pitting the Dominican people against the "Haitian threat." Rallying anti-Haitian nationalism not only unites the people but also defuses lower-class threats.

Fifth, there is a schism between "official" explanations of race relations and the reality. The case of the Dominican Republic seems to be a foreboding of the complexities of racial conflict: while Dominican elites constantly tried by different means to reproduce and impose their racist views on the larger society, the Dominican people have also widely and selectively "accepted" only some of these ideas. Moreover, these views have had a partial acceptance among lower-class Dominicans by "empowering" them with a fictitious racial-cultural superiority over Haitian immigrants.

Finally, the conceptions of race used in the study of ethnic conflict are typically Eurocentric and not always applicable in the Latin American case, where race (*raza*) tends to be confused with nation or people (for example, the Dominican people belong to the same raza, but they may have different skin colors; see Derby 1994, 490 n. 4). Though comparisons can be established, terms and their meanings are not always interchangeable. This book hopes to correct these inadequacies and to contribute to a better understanding of elites' manipulation of race in ethnic conflict and of authoritarian regime maintenance in poor countries which were reshaped or created by European colonialism.

Research Methodologies

This work examines antihaitianismo ideology by using the two approaches discussed above, the sociohistorical approach and the individual-level approach, both of which demanded different methodologies to generate evidence. In order to be consistent with the works discussed in the previous section, I tried to follow their methodologies to the greatest extent possible. The sociohistorical approach employs an interdisciplinary methodology that is characterized by its emphasis on the study of a nation's history, politics, culture, and society. Therefore, it is mostly based on the examination of written materials (books, articles, documents) regarding those issues and, as is the case in the work of van Dijk (1987), on field interviews. In contrast, the individual-level approach is based exclusively on interviews.

The first research strategy for this work consisted of library research and participant observation. Given the broad scope of the Haitian-Dominican relationship, its study requires a thorough examination of the literature on Haitian-Dominican relations, as well as an in-depth analysis of contemporary issues, such as the social, economic, political, historical, cultural, racial, and ecological issues of the Haitian-Dominican relationship. The main part of the library research on these issues was conducted during a two-year period at the University of Florida's Latin American collection, which has particularly strong holdings on the Caribbean area. This research was complemented with my own sources, which include rare or unpublished works not available outside the Dominican Republic (for example, Ginebra 1940). The bibliography at the end of this book contains some of the over eight hundred references on Haiti and the Dominican Republic that I have examined and cataloged myself in a database program. The remainder of the library research was completed in the Dominican Republic and New York City, using library sources and newspaper archives. Libraries consulted in the Dominican Republic included the Biblioteca Nacional de la República Dominicana, the library of the Banco Central de la República Dominicana, the library of the Dirección General de Migración, the Dominican Collection at the Universidad Autónoma de Santo Domingo, the libraries of the Pontificia Universidad Católica Madre y Maestra in Santiago and Santo Domingo, and the Archivo General de la Nación. In New York City, I used the libraries of the City University of New York, the New York Public Library, New York University, and Columbia University. Newspaper articles, from dailies or weeklies such as *El Siglo, El Listín Diario, El Nacional, El Sol, Última Hora, Haïti-Observateur,* the *New York Times,* and other Dominican and foreign newspapers, were also examined.

Dominican history textbooks, particularly those sections that deal with the Haitian theme, are also important sources for the study of the origin of attitudes. Education is a fundamental part of the socialization process (Orum 1983, 267–69), and most educated Dominicans (even college students) draw their knowledge of Haiti and Haitians from their history or social studies courses. I examined history textbooks dating as far back as the early twentieth century to study their anti-Haitian biases. An analysis of those particular sections dealing with Haiti revealed what Dominicans learned (or still learn) about the Haitian people in school.

Another research strategy consisted of participant observation and personal assessment. It involved several visits to the three regions of major interaction between Haitians and Dominicans: the borderlands (two Dominican villages at the southern part of the Haitian-Dominican border), the sugar industry (a state-owned sugar plantation in the southwest), and the cities of Santo Domingo and Santiago (particularly on construction sites). In these areas, I examined the nature and daily manifestations of the Haitian-Dominican relationship on a personal level, which helped me get a "feel" for my research topic. In each of the regions I interviewed dozens of people. Participant observation has long been one of the favorite research tools of anthropologists and sociologists, and it is still considered one of the basic research devices of the social scientist doing fieldwork.

Another research strategy was to interview elites. Elites in the Dominican Republic are a relatively small group, but they have had a great influence on the creation and reproduction of anti-Haitian attitudes (A. B. Betances 1985; L. Despradel 1974; F. J. Franco 1973). In the Dominican Republic, elites control policy making and the media, thus exerting considerable influence on public opinion. Therefore, beliefs, opinions, and ideologies held by Dominican elites permeate popular opinion by way of the media and authoritarian power structures.

I conducted semistructured interviews with members of the Dominican elites, such as politicians, government officials, journalists, media figures (of the printed and broadcast media), military officers, educators, and intellectuals. The semistructured interview format consisted of a set of eight to ten open-ended questions that were administered in twenty to thirty minutes, more if necessary. Of course, a longer time frame and additional questions are always more desirable, but lengthy interviews tend to become repetitive and many of my subjects had limited time. The semistructured format differs from the structured interview in that it allows for more leeway in responses while maintaining a coherent, ordered pattern of questions. Questions do not have to follow a precise order, as long as one is getting the desired information; one can always go back later to the unanswered ones. Also, the use of open-ended questions allows for further, more precise inquiries when additional information is needed (Peabody and others 1990).

Interviews with thirty-one Dominican elites were conducted in Spanish. The interviews were recorded when possible, and confidentiality for all sources was assured. The following questions were typically asked during the interviews:

1. What do you understand by *el problema haitiano* (the Haitian problem)? Is it really a problem for the Dominican Republic?
2. Of all aspects of the Haitian-Dominican relationship, which one do you think affects the Dominican Republic the most?
3. Is Haitian migration a problem? Do Haitian migrants displace Dominican workers? Are Haitian migrants an asset or a burden to the Dominican economy?

4. Is commerce with Haiti beneficial or detrimental to the Dominican economy? What about food exports to Haiti? What about contraband?

5. How does Haiti's environmental degradation concern the Dominican Republic?

6. Is the Haitian way of life a menace to Dominican society? In what way?

7. Are Haitian migrants a threat to the racial make-up of the Dominican people? In what way?

8. What are the political implications of the Haitian presence?

9. Is the border secure? Is the Dominican Republic in danger of losing territory to Haiti?

10. Are Haitian workers vital to the Dominican sugar industry? What about other crops (coffee, rice, et cetera)?

11. What do you think is the main cause of antihaitianismo in the Dominican Republic?

12. Do you think Haiti and the Dominican Republic can forget their historical differences?

13. Do you think the Dominican people are threatened by the Haitian presence? Do you feel personally threatened in any way by the Haitian presence?

14a. Should Haitians in the Dominican Republic be awarded Dominican citizenship? What about their children born here?

14b. Will migration decrease with greater control at the border?

14c. Should Haitians be forcibly repatriated?

Questions 5, 9, 10, and 12 were asked only when time allowed, as I tried not to extend the interviews for more than thirty minutes. These interviews were carried out during extended visits to the Dominican Republic in 1989, 1993, 1994, 1995, and 1997.

Finally, I conducted focus group interviews with local people in the three regions of Haitian-Dominican interaction mentioned above: the borderlands, the sugar industry, and the cities of Santo Domingo and Santiago. The focus group methodology consisted of the selection of seven to ten participants, who were given a couple of "topics" (sometimes in the form of questions) and then allowed to discuss their experiences, feelings, and reactions in a group setting. It has been defined as "a carefully planned discussion designed to obtain perceptions on a defined area of interest in a permissive, nonthreatening environment" (Krueger 1988, 18).

In my research I was interested in perceptions of the Haitian-Dominican relationship: attitudes, stereotypes, and prejudices. The following questions were asked at the beginning of each of the fifteen focus group interviews:

1. How do you get along with Haitians?
2. How do you think Haitians living in the *bateyes*/borderlands/ cities (depending on the location) are treated?[5] Why?
3. And what about Haitians living in other parts of the country? Why?

The respondents were then allowed to openly debate these issues among themselves. The discussions usually extended for over an hour, but all lasted less than two hours.

I restricted my groups to lower-class and lower-middle-class Dominicans, as they represent the majority of the population. Groups included both sexes, as well as different age groups. Participants were selected on location (convenience sampling), a technique substantiated by the literature on focus groups (Krueger 1988, 96) and dictated by field realities. I resided in these lower-class communities for days at a time, getting to know many of the respondents outside the interview context. Most of the focus group interviews were carried out in the summer of 1989, at a time when the Dominican Republic was facing a deep economic crisis.[6] There was no diplomatic crisis with Haiti nor any large-scale deportations of Haitian migrants going on at the time (that is, there were no national events that could have influenced the nature of the responses).

Most of the focus group interviews were held in the backyards of homes or under large trees in the field, so that a fairly large group (of up to ten respondents) could assemble and talk in a relaxed atmosphere. I provided the respondents with drinks and snacks to further encourage a mood of open rapport and discussion of ideas. Again, the interviews were recorded, and the participants' confidentiality was assured. The data collected in the focus group interviews was qualitative in nature and will be used to illustrate the nature and diversity of anti-Haitian attitudes among Dominicans.

In conclusion, for my research I developed a methodology that combined the perceptions of the nations' leaders (through elite interviews and literary sources) with those of the everyday citizen (through focus group interviews and participant observation). This qualitative data will be used for three purposes: first, to document the presence of antihaitianismo at both the elite and the popular levels; second, to illustrate that prejudice is not an individual but a social phenomenon; and third, to show how Dominican elites have utilized antihaitianismo ideology for political purposes.

This book is an examination of a Caribbean phenomenon, of an ideological apartheid within the confines of a small island. It is a book about elites and the exercise of power, a dominant ideology, and the history of two nations: Haiti and the Dominican Republic. It offers an analysis of how ideologies and history have influenced each other—for ideas cannot be separated from their sociohistorical context—and in turn how events have influenced and shaped the development of antihaitianismo ideology by Dominican elites.

The Dominican Republic is a good case study of the deliberate manipulation of racial prejudice and nationalism by elites bent on promoting their own definition of nationhood and on maintaining their hold on political and economic power. The country highlights the importance of examining elites' manipulation of racist nationalism in the management of communal conflict, as a factor in the elites' own access and control over the political arena. This dominant ideology is more than simply the prejudiced response of elites to a particular insular situation. Parallels with other societies are evident—particularly in the Hispanic Caribbean—as most of the ideas used by antihaitianismo ideology were imported. Dominican elites did not live in isolation; their prejudiced ideas were in part the result of a racist colonial heritage and the adaptation of foreign ideas to the Dominican Republic.

Chapter 1 is an examination of the colonial and early republican origins of antihaitianismo ideology. One of the main arguments of the chapter is that antihaitianismo has its origins in the racial prejudices of Spanish colonial society in Santo Domingo. Even before there was a Haiti, the roots of antihaitianismo ideology had been planted by the Spanish. The chapter also examines the conflictive relationship between Haiti and the Dominican Republic in the mid–nineteenth century, and the development of a national myth—under the influence of foreign ideologies—by Dominican elites in the late nineteenth century. Finally, the chapter looks at political and economic changes in the Dominican Republic at the turn of the century, such as the development of the sugar industry and the U.S. military occupation (1916–24), which brought about important changes in the way Dominican elites looked at the "national problem" and redefined antihaitianismo ideology.

Chapters 2 and 3 are devoted to the zenith of antihaitianismo ideology: the Trujillo era (1930–61). The dictatorship of General Rafael Trujillo used antihaitianismo for propaganda purposes and made it into a state-sponsored ideology. Chapter 2 examines how Trujillo used intellectuals to transform antihaitianismo into a coherent, powerful ideology, while chapter 3 details how these ideas were backed up with the power and resources of the *Trujillista* state. Moreover, Trujillo deliberately unleashed "waves" of antihaitianismo in times of diplomatic tensions with Haiti, such as right after the 1937 massacre. Finally, chapter 3 also analyzes how antihaitianismo ideology penetrated the national psyche, after years of bombardment by official anti-Haitian propaganda.

Chapter 4 details the redefinition of antihaitianismo ideology after the death of Trujillo. It analyzes neoantihaitianismo by looking at the texts that have sought to transform antihaitianismo into an ideology more in tune with contemporary issues, and examines how antihaitianismo ideology is still being reproduced among the Dominican people through the socialization process. The roles of history texts and the media are stressed as powerful agents of socialization. Finally, the chapter examines evidence of the presence and extent of antihaitianismo among the Dominican people by looking at focus group interviews, individual interviews, and surveys. The most salient issues mentioned by respondents are discussed, as well as the difficulties and pitfalls of measuring the sociopolitical impact of antihaitianismo ideology in the Dominican Republic.

Chapter 5 examines Haitian-Dominican relations in the post-Trujillo period, concentrating on the interplay between antihaitianismo ideology and domestic and external policies. It argues that foreign policy toward Haiti is often a reflection of Dominican domestic politics. The chapter concludes by looking at the most conspicuous contemporary political use of antihaitianismo: the "dirty campaign" against presidential candidate José F. Peña Gómez, whom his political opponents accused of being of Haitian origin.

The conclusion reassesses some of the main issues presented in the book and analyzes the future outlook for antihaitianismo ideology and its potential consequences for the Dominican Republic. It also reexamines some of the theoretical issues raised earlier in the volume.

With this work, I hope to draw attention to the particular case of the Dominican Republic, where Hispanophile elites have fabricated a dominant—though contested—myth of racial nationhood vis-à-vis neighboring Haiti. Moreover, I want to shed light on the particular nature of socioracial relations in the Hispanic Caribbean—a region far from free of racism. And finally, I hope that the examination of the Dominican case will offer new insights into the complexity of ethnic conflict and the ways it can be manipulated for political gain.

1

Antihaitianismo

From Colonialism to the Twentieth Century

Antihaitianismo ideology is the manifestation of the long-term evolution of racial prejudices, the selective interpretation of historical facts, and the creation of a nationalist Dominican "false consciousness." The formation of this ideology did not take place spontaneously; it was orchestrated by powerful elite groups with strong interests to defend. Race and class had been closely intertwined issues since the creation of the Spanish colony of Santo Domingo. Later, when the Dominican Republic achieved its independence in 1844, the racial issue played an important role in the elite-led development of feelings and concepts of nationhood. Moreover, Dominican elites tried to impose their ideas over competing, alternative "popular" notions of *dominicanidad* (Dominicanness)—in some cases very successfully.

How this attempt at "national image building" and attempted definition and diffusion took place is the focus of this chapter. The first section examines the role played by the Spanish colonial regime in the creation and reproduction of prejudice and racism directed against the colony's groups of color (first against the Taíno Indians and mestizos, then against blacks and mulattos). These prejudices, along with the socioeconomic differentiation evident in the two sides of the island, eventually led to the formulation of anti-Haitian attitudes after the creation of the Republic of Haiti in 1804. The second section analyzes the development of antihaitianismo ideology during the republican era—up to 1930, the beginning of the Trujillo era. It examines how Dominican elites used "popular" culture, socioeconomic and racial differences, imported ideologies, and particularly the manipulation of history to develop a number of myths and prejudices regarding Haitians and the Dominican Republic. These ideas became the foundation for the dominant ideology of antihaitianismo.

The Colonial Origins of Antihaitianismo

The early origins of what later came to be known as antihaitianismo are to be found in the racial prejudices of the inhabitants of the Spanish colony of Santo Domingo. After Columbus discovered the island that he named La Española (Hispaniola) in 1492, the colony of Santo Domingo was the center of the expanding Spanish empire in the New World, until it was displaced by Cuba in the sixteenth century. The Spanish found a Stone Age culture inhabiting the island, the Taíno Indians, and gold. Both were depleted in a couple of generations. The Spanish, who had just finished a centuries-long struggle against the Moors, believed that they were subduing a barbaric, idol-worshiping people, deemed suitable only for servitude (Tolentino Dipp 1992, chaps. 1, 2). The lack of white women in the colony led to the birth of the first mestizos, the offspring of Indians and Spaniards. The mestizos were also subjected to the same prejudices as the Taínos, though to a lesser degree. This early form of racial prejudice was short-lived, however, due to the extinction of the Taínos. Attempts to replace them with Indians from other islands (such as the Lucayos from the Bahamas) were unsuccessful; they also died quickly.

With the disappearance of gold and the Indian labor force, the colony entered into a period of crisis. The crisis was temporarily palliated with the introduction of sugarcane cultivation and slavery. Africans slaves became the perfect replacement for the Indians. Before the advent of the plantation system, black slaves had not been perceived by Europeans as very different from Indians. But their use in sugar plantations led to the creation of racial prejudices among Europeans in order to justify the exploitation of black human beings by labeling them as "inferior" (Williams 1984). Even moral characteristics—such as laziness, dishonesty, and intellectual inferiority—were biologically attributed to blacks, based solely on their skin color (Deive 1976, 76–77). Even though the sugar plantation system only lasted until the late sixteenth century in Santo Domingo, the racial prejudices and racist social structures created by the colonial administration remained in place for centuries, particularly among the white colonial upper classes.

For almost three centuries, the political and social structures in the colony of Santo Domingo were not unlike those in the other Spanish colonies in the Caribbean. The white Spanish elite controlled the colony's administration and ruled over a racially mixed population of Creoles and slaves. Still, Santo Domingo's colonial society, given the influence of a generalized economic backwardness that tended to mitigate class tensions and reduce social distances, was probably more egalitarian than neighboring Cuba, the seat of Spanish power in the Caribbean. By the seventeenth century, Santo Domingo's main economic activity was cattle ranching, which lessened racial tensions and even promoted miscegenation. But slaves were not treated as equals in that colony. They were mistreated, and slave rebellions were severely punished in a colonial society where skin color still indicated—to a large degree—one's social standing and economic position (Tolentino Dipp 1973, 1992).

In colonial Santo Domingo there was a close relationship between economic activities and the treatment of slaves. Domestic slaves, as well as those in the cattle-ranching sector, were less exploited than slaves on sugar plantations. The economic activity in which the slave was utilized shaped the kind—and degree—of exploitation. A sugar plantation was a capitalist, agro-exporting operation that required coercive force to maintain a profitable level of production. Cattle ranching, on the other hand, was a semi-feudal, pastoral activity in which both slaves and owners had a great deal of free time. Thus the fact that sugar had been replaced by cattle ranching as the main economic activity of Santo Domingo by the seventeenth century determined the nature of slavery in Santo Domingo during the next two centuries (Mejía Ricart 1985, 64–67). The fact that Santo Domingo became a poor, sparsely populated, cattle-ranching colony determined that slavery operated in a generally less exploitative form than in neighboring French Saint-Domingue, for example.[1]

Furthermore, the generalized poverty of the colony and its intrinsic characteristics had other consequences. First, fewer slaves were imported into the colony of Santo Domingo (because few people could afford to buy them) than into other colonies, such as Cuba and Saint-Domingue. As a result, most slaves in Santo Domingo were born and raised in the colony. Second, the average ratio of slaves to freemen remained small. Third, slave owners (who could not easily afford to replace slaves) had to take better care of them.[2] Fourth, blacks, and particularly mulattos, often occupied midlevel administrative positions usually reserved for whites. The colonial history of Santo Domingo is full of examples of special royal "concessions" allowing a mulatto to occupy a "whites only" position, given the lack of white men in the colony (Deive 1980; Utrera 1978). And fifth, miscegenation, particularly among the large, lower-class majority of the population, became the norm. Again, these events were not the result of Spanish racial ideals (which remained very discriminatory), but of the socioeconomic realities of the colony of Santo Domingo. While the Spanish authorities and colonial elites dreamed of a racially pure society, there was really little that they could do to stop the interbreeding of whites, blacks, and mulattos in this colonial backwater of the Spanish empire. With the possible exception of the white upper classes, the colonists of Santo Domingo freely mixed, giving way by the eighteenth century to the first major mulatto community in the world (Pérez Cabral 1967).

The rapid growth of the French colony of Saint-Domingue in the western part of the island during the seventeenth and eighteenth centuries altered Santo Domingo's colonial status quo. With half a million slaves and a far stronger agro-exporting economy, the French colony changed forever the destiny of Spanish Santo Domingo (Knight 1990). The Spanish authorities and other colonial elites fought for decades to maintain the political and cultural integrity of their territory, but to no avail. As a consequence, the first glimpses of Dominican nationalism emerged in the eighteenth century as part of a struggle in which Dominicans sought to differentiate themselves from the French (Pierre-Charles 1974, 28). In the elites' view, the inhabitants of Santo Domingo considered themselves as Catholic, loyal Spanish subjects fighting against the encroachment of the French, Spain's European enemy. Furthermore, all the inhabitants of the western part of Hispaniola—including blacks and mulattos—were considered "French" by the people of Santo Domingo. These ideas led to the development of a dual prejudice against the people of the west: a national-cultural prejudice against "French" culture and civilization (which were

Map 1. Treaty of Aranjuez, 1777

considered alien and different), topped by a racial prejudice against the non-European population of the west (which was considered twice as inferior—culturally and racially).

These cultural and racial prejudices were so generalized among the people of the colony of Santo Domingo that even slaves shared them (Barskett [1818] 1971, 188). The slaves of the east considered themselves superior to the slaves of the west, by the simple fact that they possessed a Hispanic culture. Foreign visitors to Santo Domingo were surprised—not to mention amused—by the fact that blacks referred to their western neighbors as "those Negroes" (Mackenzie [1830] 1971, 215). Also, most slaves in Santo Domingo were *ladino*—or Creole—slaves, born and raised in the colony. The extremely high death rates among slaves in Saint-Domingue (as high as 10 percent per year), on the other hand, meant that most slaves in the French colony were *bozales,* or recently brought from Africa (Rogoziński 1994, 139).

Periods of peace in the periodic wars in Europe led to the development of trade between the two colonies. The French colony—with its plantation economy—required a large number of heads of cattle to feed its slave population, for transportation, and as animal power in the mills. The Spanish colony, underpopulated and with wide ranges full of roaming cattle, became the main supplier of cattle to Saint-Domingue. In turn, the Spanish colonists acquired much-needed European products that Spain could not supply. Trade with Saint-Domingue, of course, was not always legal or stable. War and the Spanish authorities curtailed the trade on several occasions but could not stop it completely (Moreau de Saint-Méry [1796] 1944, 359–92). During the eighteenth century, the Spanish authorities taxed the trade, which added a considerable income to the coffers of the local colonial administration. In 1777, the Spanish Crown legally recognized the French colony (by the Treaty of Aranjuez), and the first formal border between the two colonies was established (see map 1). The colonial status quo would probably have continued had it not been for an event that drastically changed the face of the Caribbean forever: the Haitian Revolution.

In 1789, the repercussions of the French Revolution made themselves felt at the colony. The three ruling minorities (*grand blancs* [wealthy whites], *petits blancs* [poor whites], and the *gens de couleur* [mulattos]) rallied behind the Revolution's motto of "Liberty, Equality, and Fraternity," though each one for its own reasons. The grand blancs wanted autonomy, while the petits blancs and the gens de couleur demanded equality with the richer group. The petits blancs wanted more political and economic equality, while the gens de couleur wanted racial equality. Demands increased, and with them, conflict. Soon all three groups were mobilizing their slaves as troops for their cause. At one point, however, things got out of control. The slaves, realizing their strength in numbers, revolted in 1791. What began as a conflict between elites turned into the largest slave revolt in history. Chaos soon engulfed Saint-Domingue. The slaves, under the direction of Toussaint Louverture, an ex-slave himself, defeated the white and mulatto armies in a bloody ten-year struggle that destroyed the colony's economic infrastructure. After Toussaint's imprisonment and deportation to France, Jean-Jacques Dessalines took over the struggle, finally realizing the independence of the Republic of Haiti on 1 January 1804.

The ex-slaves' struggle for liberty was not a simple war of independence, like those that were to follow in Latin America during the nineteenth century, but a true social revolution, the first one of the Americas. As such, it had traumatic effects on the country. The plantation system, based exclusively on the exploitation of slave labor, collapsed. The white ruling elites, and even some of the gens de couleur, were massacred or driven away and replaced by blacks and mulattos. And the colonial administration gave way to an independent republic. In all these three aspects—society, the economy, and politics—revolutionary changes were effected through the use of high levels of violence.

All these events, of course, had not gone unnoticed in Spanish Santo

Domingo. When fighting against the French, Toussaint sought refuge in the Spanish colony, and even fought along with the Spanish for some time, before finally turning against them for their continuing support of slavery (Korngold 1965, 95–107). The Spanish colony also supplied the huge amounts of cattle that the war effort demanded. Food became scarce in Saint-Domingue as a result of both the lack of slave labor to grow crops and the slaves' guerrilla tactics of burning the fields to starve the French. French refugees arrived in Santo Domingo with horrifying accounts of massacres and racial strife. Finally, Spanish Santo Domingo became fully involved in the Haitian Revolution when it was ceded to France in 1795.

Spain, after having been defeated by France in Europe, had to cede its Santo Domingo colony to the French in order to regain the territory that it had lost in the Iberian peninsula during the war (Peña Batlle [1946] 1988, 100–101). The cession was rendered official by the Treaty of Basel in 1795. However, the French had no way of occupying Santo Domingo. They could not even control their own colony of Saint-Domingue, then under the effective control of Toussaint. It was Toussaint himself who finally enforced the Treaty of Basel, occupying with his troops the former Spanish colony in 1801 (Peña Batlle [1946] 1988, 102–3). The Spanish and the French, in particular Napoleon Bonaparte, tried to delay Toussaint, but to no avail. Napoleon—who did not trust Toussaint—wanted a white French army to occupy Santo Domingo, not Toussaint's black army.

To the elites of Santo Domingo, who were well aware of the chaotic situation in Saint-Domingue and the plight of the former white masters, the presence of Toussaint's black troops was horrifying. The Santo Domingo elites did not particularly like the French, but they feared Toussaint's black troops—and his actions—even more. For example, Toussaint proclaimed the abolition of slavery in the formerly Spanish colony. Even though slavery did not have in Santo Domingo the economic importance that it had had in Saint-Domingue, the Santo Domingo elite considered slavery a basic institution of Spanish society (and one that helped perpetuate racial stratification). Many upper-class families decided to leave the island and moved to the Spanish possessions of Cuba, Venezuela, and Puerto Rico, both before and after the arrival of Toussaint's army (García [1878] 1968, 1:287).

When the independence of the Republic of Haiti was declared in 1804, there remained little of the original French army in Santo Domingo. French general Louis Ferrand, however, decided not to surrender. He took over

Santo Domingo city and prepared it for a long siege. The expected Haitian invasion came in 1805, when Dessalines decided to reannex the eastern part of the island. For three weeks Dessalines laid siege to the city of Santo Domingo but had to abandon it when French ships appeared on the horizon (Lemonnier-Delafosse [1846] 1946, 116–17).

During their retreat, however, the Haitian armies left a trail of blood. They ransacked all the towns in their path, killing many of their inhabitants. According to Haitian historian Price-Mars: "And so it was that the retreat of the Haitian army was one of the most dramatic and bloodiest episodes of a dramatic and bloody history. Burnings of farms, destructions of cattle, execution of hostages, arrests of women and children, the brutal transfer of them to the West, after the army; nothing was missing in such a sad portrait of futile horrors. For Dessalines, the people of the East resembled the French whites, his eternal enemies" ([1953] 1958, 1:97–98). Dessalines, furious over being unable to capture Santo Domingo, and believing a French invasion to be imminent, reverted to the "scorched earth" policy that he had successfully used during the Haitian Revolution. Furthermore, Dessalines now considered the Santo Domingo colonists, who had preferred to side with the French, as his enemies. His bloody military campaign had traumatic effects on the Santo Domingo colonists, developing a strong anti-Haitian resentment among them that lasted for years.

When Haiti became an independent state in 1804, the "undesirable" traits of French culture and the French Revolution were transplanted to the Haitian revolutionaries in the minds of the Santo Domingo elites. The Hispanic nationalism of the Santo Domingo elites not only persisted but was reinforced by the horrors of the Haitian Revolution and the brutal campaign of Dessalines against Santo Domingo in 1805.[3] They did not just see their people as different from their western neighbors; they preferred to be anything else before being Haitian. These feelings were conceived and reproduced by the colonial elites, who sought to maintain Spain's sovereignty, even though the colony had been ceded to France in 1795. In spite of that, the colonists of Santo Domingo grudgingly preferred to be ruled by white Frenchmen than by black Haitians. To promote nationalist feelings, elites emphasized the "Spanishness" of the Santo Domingo colonists versus the French, and later, the Haitians. Like the Spanish, the elites of Santo Domingo thought that they were white (at least somatically speaking), Catholic, and had a Hispanic culture. The Haitians, on the other hand, represented for them the opposite (and the worst of traits): they were black, they practiced voodoo,[4] and they had an African culture with a thin French veneer. Apparently, these feelings had become so widespread by the early nineteenth century that the Santo Domingo colonists, regardless of their color, used to commonly refer to themselves as *blancos de la tierra,*[5] that is, "whites of the land," because they had been born Creole and not African (Lemonnier-Delafosse [1846] 1946, 151).

The Catholic Church played a particularly important role in the development of these prejudices. The clergy, mostly composed of Spaniards, reproduced among the Santo Domingo colonists their racial views and their animosity toward the secular ideas of the French Revolution.[6] As respected members of their communities and with an undisputed moral authority, Catholic priests molded the values and attitudes of their faithful (Pérez Memén 1987, 195). From the pulpit and through daily interaction with their communities, Catholic priests instilled white Hispanic values in the colonists, even among the black and mulatto lower classes, which made up the majority of the population.

The Spanish values of the Santo Domingo elites were so deeply ingrained in them that after expelling the French in 1809, the colony was voluntarily reverted to the Spanish Crown. At a time when rebellions were erupting throughout the mainland Spanish colonies, Santo Domingo remained firmly attached to the Crown. By 1821, however, the ineptitude of the Spanish administration had forced the elites of Santo Domingo to search for other political alternatives, but without losing their Hispanic values and prejudiced attitudes. Paradoxically, while most of the lower classes favored annexation to Haiti (admired for its republican institutions and egalitarian society), the white Hispanic elites of Santo Domingo sought to become a part of Gran Colombia.

The elite's political project was unrealistic and short-lived. In 1822, Haitian president Jean-Pierre Boyer annexed the eastern part of the island, declaring it part of the Republic of Haiti. Slavery was reabolished (after having been reimposed by the French), and the inhabitants of the east were fully integrated as Haitian citizens. But the Santo Domingo elites remained firmly attached to their prejudiced worldview. José Núñez de Cáceres, the architect of the ephemeral independence of 1821, had to bow to the power and popularity of Haitian president Jean-Pierre Boyer, but not without first warning him of what he perceived as the abysmal differences between Haitians and the Hispanic colonists of Santo Domingo. Such differences, according to Núñez de Cáceres, represented "a wall as natural and unsurpassable as the material interposition of the Alps and the Pyrenees" (García [1878] 1968, 2:88).

The Haitian occupation (1822–44), though passively accepted by most of the population (and even celebrated by lower-class groups), was strongly rejected by the Hispanic elites, who lost some of their privileges and administrative jobs to the occupation forces and lower-class blacks and mulattos. The elites further resented being at the mercy of individuals whom they considered inferior, due to their skin color and social status. The majority of Haitian army officers were ex-slaves themselves, with little or no education, and lacking the finesse and manners that elites regarded so highly. During the period of the Haitian occupation, many of these elite families left the country, a fact deplored by Hispanophile historians, who commented that Santo Domingo lost most of its "best" families at that time (Balaguer 1984, 59–60.).

The Catholic Church also opposed the Haitian occupation on cultural and racial grounds, particularly given the secular orientation of the Haitian administration. Church properties were expropriated, and Spanish clergy were expelled by the Haitian authorities or left the country in disgust, which led to the closing of the university for lack of a teaching staff and governmental indolence (Baur 1947, 319). Still, the Catholic Church remained an influential force in Santo Domingo.

By the early 1840s, the population of Hispaniola had grown tired of Boyer and his failed policies. Some laws, like the 1826 Rural Code, the imposition of the French language, the breakdown of large cattle estates, and the taxes required to pay a large indemnity to France, became very unpopular measures. The behavior of Haitian troops often contributed to the increasing disappointment of Dominicans. Even Haitian historians have criticized the misguided policies of the Haitian occupation. Dantès Bellegarde, for example, mentions how the Haitian military treated the Dominican people in a despotic way, like "a conquered country" (1953, 131).

Boyer faced innumerable obstacles—and the scorn of many Dominicans—when he tried to realize his dream of one nation in one island. In 1843, what began as a reform movement in the west acquired revolutionary connotations in the east. Not only had the Haitian occupation failed economically, but it had also failed to create cultural and emotional bonds between Haitians and Dominicans. Boyer himself acknowledged that fact, and it was customary for Haitians to still refer to the inhabitants of the east as "Spaniards" (Madiou [1847] 1981, 8:90). The economic decline of the Haitian nation, plus the cultural differences between Haitians and Dominicans—exacerbated by the anti-Haitian ideology of the Hispanic elites—led to the formation of separatist movements in the east.

Most of these elite-led movements sought the separation of Santo Domingo from Haiti and the protection of a foreign power, plus the maintenance of Hispanic values and the preservation of elite privileges. Even the liberal conspiracy led by Juan Pablo Duarte sought to defend Hispanic values, as it was initially organized by the white, upper-middle-class, urban youth of the city of Santo Domingo (A. Despradel 1976, 34). Duarte and his followers, for example, adopted Christian symbols and slogans for their secret society La Trinitaria (named after the Holy Trinity) and designed the Dominican flag with a white cross in the center as a symbol of their Catholic faith (García [1878] 1968, 2:225). On 27 February 1844, the expected rebellion took place. The rebels took the city of Santo Domingo and forced the Haitian authorities to capitulate. In about fifteen days, the rest of the country joined the rebel forces and declared its separation from Haiti. It was only through the integration of black figures into the movement—such as Francisco Sánchez del Rosario and José Joaquín Puello—and its strong position against slavery that the black masses supported the struggle for Dominican independence, for they feared the reestablishment of slavery if Santo Domingo became separated from Haiti.[7]

The Search for a National Identity

When the Dominican Republic finally achieved its independence, its elites portrayed this event as the culmination of their efforts to maintain Hispanic-Catholic culture intact in the face of the Haitian occupation. As they put it in the independence manifesto of the Dominican Republic, "Due to the difference of customs and the rivalry that exists between ones and the others [referring to Haiti and the Dominican Republic], there will never be a perfect union nor harmony" (L. Despradel 1974, 86). With the Haitians out of the picture, Dominican elites regained their privileged social position and their high-level administrative posts. Duarte and his followers, who led the only truly liberal-minded movement, were quickly driven from the political scene by conservative forces.[8]

The Haitian-Dominican wars to consolidate Dominican independence fostered nationalist, anti-Haitian attitudes among the Dominican people. In the face of repeated Haitian attempts to recover their former territory, the presence of antihaitianismo among the general Dominican population of the mid–nineteenth century is understandable. The independence struggle was often expressed in an anti-Haitian form. What is more difficult to understand is the extension of these prejudices to black Dominicans and the perpetuation of anti-Haitian attitudes well after independence. The struggle against Haiti exacerbated racial prejudices in the newly born Dominican Republic. Dominican elites considered blacks a potential "fifth column," particularly after their initial distrust of the separatist movement. It was believed that black Dominicans were prone to identify with Haiti as a result of their skin color. Thus it was not surprising that before going into battle, military leaders warned their troops: "Whoever is black better speak clearly" (Balcácer 1977, 26). There also were at least two well-documented cases of political trials and executions carried out against Dominican "Negrophiles," most notably the Puello brothers (Veloz Maggiolo 1996), during the 1840s.

Dominican elites also used antihaitianismo ideology to cloak their annexationist ideas. Even though the Dominican armies were never defeated by Haiti, Dominican elites proposed annexation to a foreign power as the only solution to protect the Dominican Republic. These elites—who clearly had no nationalist vocation—used "the Haitian scare" to further their political agendas. They did not believe that the Dominican Republic was a viable country, plus they had economic interests that would be furthered by an annexation (Jimenes Grullón 1969, 69). Over the next thirty years, leaders like Pedro Santana and Buenaventura Báez developed all sorts of schemes to seek the annexation of the Dominican Republic to Spain, France, England, and the United States (Martínez-Fernández 1993). Their arguments ranged from military security to economic necessity to plainly racist ideas. Báez—a dark mulatto himself and the son of a slave woman—wrote to the French government: "Europe, which is the center of civilization, must convince itself that Dominicans currently constitute the only check against the cruelty and the incursions of the black race. A word from your government and the country will be entirely yours" (Heneken [1852] 1959, 438). In another letter, he added, "We are not racially pure whites, but we will never tolerate being ruled by blacks" (Sang Ben 1991, 53).[9] Foreign promoters of annexation shared these racist ideas and argued to their governments, "And in this preponderance of the white population consists the superiority of the Dominican Republic over the Haitian [population]" (Rodríguez Demorizi 1959, 112). Thus "the Haitian scare" had no military basis; it was only the reflection of the anti-Haitian prejudices of Dominican elites and their foreign mentors.

The Haitian-Dominican wars also led to the creation of myths that sought to support the presumed inferiority of Haitians vis-à-vis Dominicans. The military victories of the Dominican armies—smaller in number—were interpreted not as the result of sound military tactics but as the intervention of "the Divine Providence whose almighty arm is visible on all occasions," because God defended the Dominican Republic from "those bloody monsters" (Rodríguez Demorizi 1946, 182–83). Regardless of this "divine-sponsored" invincibility, Dominican elites—for the reasons mentioned above—continued with their annexationist plans, eventually culminating in the reannexation of the country to Spain in 1861, through the efforts of "the Liberator" and military hero General Pedro Santana.

The reannexation to Spain marks the high point of the pro-Hispanic elites and their antihaitianismo ideology. Spain, the colonial motherland, was considered by some elite sectors (particularly the cattle ranchers) as the perfect protector from Haiti, even though by this time the Haitian leadership no longer planned to reconquer the Dominican Republic. Annexation, however, crashed against the nationalist feelings of the majority of the population, who feared a return to the aristocratic inequities of the Spanish colony and fought against it. Certainly, the national consciousness of the Dominican people was far more developed than that of its elites. By this time, a Creole culture had developed among the black and mulatto masses, particularly among the large peasant population. Even the Spanish colonial administration understood this fact and quickly came to the realization that the Dominican and Spanish people were fundamentally different (Landolfi 1981, chap. 4).

The pro-Hispanic elites, however, insisted on their utopian project at all costs. General Santana himself, for example, was appointed "Marquis of Las Carreras" by the Spanish government. Sánchez, the Trinitario and one of the founding fathers of the Dominican Republic, was captured during the early stages of the struggle and executed.[10] The ill-fated annexation was over by 1865, and Spain lost its prestige in the eyes of the Dominican people.

To the surprise of Haiti's detractors, the administration of Haitian president Fabre-Nicolas Geffrard helped Dominican patriots in their struggle against the Spanish, providing them with refuge and supplies (Bellegarde 1953, 166–67). Haiti's leaders realized that an independent Dominican Republic was preferable to a Spanish colony next door, particularly considering that slavery had not been abolished in the Spanish colonies of Cuba and Puerto Rico. Thereafter, Haiti became an ardent defender of Dominican sovereignty, and relations between the two countries reached their best point since Dominican independence in 1844. As a result, a peace, friendship, trade, navigation, and extradition treaty was signed by both countries in 1874 (Price-Mars [1953] 1958, 3:180–82).

The last quarter of the nineteenth century was a period of intense economic changes and political infighting. The Dominican Republic became a sugar exporter and entered the global capitalist economy, finally transcending the semifeudal socioeconomic structures of the past (Cassá 1992, chap. 20). On the political scene, infighting between local caudillos increased, at least until the last decade of the century, when Ulises Heureaux established a well-entrenched dictatorship. The fluxing and uncertain state of things, the fiasco of the Spanish reannexation, the ignominious scheme of President Buenaventura Báez to annex the country to the United States in 1871,[11] and the periodic "revolutions" that rocked the country led the Dominican intelligentsia to a reexamination of their national values. Two trends—or currents—emerged from the intellectual debate on the issues of the day: *indigenismo* and pessimism. These two trends—but particularly indigenismo—redefined and reproduced the antihaitianismo ideology of the Dominican elites in accordance with the new times.

Indigenismo was a romantic literary trend that dealt with the Amerindian—or indigenous—theme. It was typical of many Latin American countries at the time, even those where Indians were rather unimportant or nonexistent, such as Uruguay (Hoetink 1994, 121) and Haiti.[12] The indigenista writers exalted the life and struggle of the Taínos, and established a symbolic link with the original inhabitants of Hispaniola. In their search for a new national identity, Dominican elites looked at their Amerindian past, given Spain's lost of prestige among the Dominican people and the coming to power of dark-skinned military leaders (such as Gregorio Luperón and Ulises Heureaux). The publication of the novel *Enriquillo* by Manuel de Jesús Galván (1882), a heroic portrayal of an Indian leader's resistance against enslavement by the Spanish colonizers, and the collection of poems *Fantasías indígenas* by José Joaquín Pérez (1877), mark the high point of the indigenista literary movement in the Dominican Republic.[13]

Even though the Amerindian population of Hispaniola was exterminated in less than a century, the pro-Hispanic Dominican elites portrayed the Dominican people as the descendants of these brave Indians and the Spanish colonists, deliberately obviating the black element in Dominican society. For most Dominicans, both the elites and the masses, it was a greater honor to have a rebellious Indian (like Enriquillo) as a predecessor than an African slave. Their fabricated Indian ancestry also created a mythological national past, with deep roots in the prehistory of the island, which gave the Dominican nation a sense of continuity and helped it repress its traumatic colonial history.[14]

It was just a matter of time before Dominican mulattos started considering themselves as *indios* (an obvious reference to their claimed Indian ancestry). The myth of the Dominican indio was the most important ethnic fabrication developed in the late nineteenth century—and remains influential to this day. Mulattos, who make up most of the Dominican population, lexically disappeared and were replaced by the Dominican indio. Being indio also helped mulattos "whiten" their own perception of their color and race (L. Despradel 1974, 94–97; Fennema and Loewenthal 1987, 28). In order to varnish their common African past, the Dominican people essentially dropped the words *black* and *mulatto* from their vocabulary and replaced them with the less traumatic and more socially desirable *indio*.[15] The terms *black* and *mulatto* were instead often used to refer to Haitians, who were considered truly black. The indio myth became so widespread that even a black nationalist leader like Gregorio Luperón referred to the mixed race of the Dominican people; a race that, by the effect of climate, would turn back into that of the original inhabitants of the island (that is, the Indians) (L. Despradel 1974, 96). More than ever, the pro-Hispanic Dominican elites felt that theirs was a unique race.

The Dominican elites still professed their anti-Haitian and antiblack prejudices, in part because they reflected their personal view of what Haiti was, and also because they employed antihaitianismo ideology as an element of national cohesion and domination. These prejudices were reproduced at the popular level, and being Dominican soon became identified with being formally anti-Haitian. The poems of José Antonio Alix expressed the antihaitianismo ideology of the elites in a popular context. For example, in his famous "Dialogue" between a Dominican peasant and a Haitian voodoo priest, the Dominican peasant repeatedly refuses to dance *bodú* (voodoo) and in the end uses his sharp machete against the stubborn Haitian—an action reminiscent of the wars of independence. In 1875, poet Félix María del Monte published in *Cantos dominicanos* the following verse, illustrative of the elites' anti-Haitian prejudices:

¿Quién tiene lazo de unión
con esos diablos sañudos
que beben sangre y desnudos
en pacto con Belzebú
bailan su horrible *bodú*
y comen muchachos crudos?

Who has ties
with those cruel devils
who drink blood and naked
in a pact with Beelzebub
dance their horrible *bodú* [voodoo]
and eat live children?

(Rodríguez Demorizi 1971, 95–97)

In this ideological worldview of the Dominican elites, Dominicans were portrayed as devout Catholics, while Haitians were voodoo sorcerers who believed in spirits and utilized black magic in mysterious ceremonies (Hoetink 1982, 181–92). Furthermore, Dominican elites thought of themselves as somatically "white," proud descendants of the Spanish conquistadors, while Haitians were the "real" blacks, the sons and daughters of African slaves.

It was not long before Dominicans of all classes—including even those who had dark skin—started considering themselves "not black." Only Haitians were considered black. Therefore, race, culture, and nation were forged into one by the Dominican elites. The Hispanic peasant from the Cibao (the lighter-skinned region of the country) and its typical merengue were eventually transformed into national symbols—particularly during the first half of the twentieth century (Austerlitz 1997, chaps. 3–4; Hoetink 1994, chap. 3). A new patriotic poetry was developed (including the current national anthem), official national symbols were established, and Dominican history was reinterpreted by nationalist historians, resurrecting old heroes and establishing the trilogy of the "Fathers of the Dominican Republic": Juan Pablo Duarte y Diez, Matías Ramón Mella y Castillo, and Francisco Sánchez del Rosario. Being Dominican was being Hispanic and not being black, regardless of one's skin tone. Not surprisingly, the American commissioner Benjamin E. Green reports earlier in the century how black Dominicans would comment: "Yes, I am a Negro, but a white Negro" (Welles 1986, 1:108).

The fabrication of a Dominican nation, along with its indio myth, was also a defensive strategy developed by an elite sector endangered by mass mobilization and foreign capitalist penetration. As contradictory as it seems, Dominican elites (like most elites throughout Latin America) constantly complained about their country's underdevelopment and called for its modernization. Development, in the form of foreign investment, however, brought with it unintended consequences such as mass mobilization and the displacement of peasant societies, new political actors, and external dependence. Even liberal intellectuals, such as Pedro F. Bonó (1980), warned against the menace of global capitalism in the form of foreign sugar plantations and believed that it would destroy the soul of the nation, that is, its peasantry. Others, like Eugenio María de Hostos and later Américo Lugo, saw it from a political perspective and warned about U.S. imperialism. Dominican elites, traditionally weak and divided against the onslaught of capitalism, felt their patriarchal power jeopardized by these developments and responded by "inventing" the Dominican nation: a romanticized, nostalgic aspiration for a culturally and racially homogenous society in a collapsing world threatened by modernization. These needs explain, for example, their romanticized notion of the campesino cibaeño and small-scale production as symbols not of the actual Dominican Republic but of what the elites wanted it to be.

Pessimism was another consequence of the Dominican elites' traumatic experience with modernization (Baud 1996, 123–25). The pessimist literary movement was originally rooted in the philosophical teachings of Eugenio María de Hostos,[16] who introduced positivism into the Dominican Republic and influenced the thought of a whole generation of Dominican intellectuals (Cassá 1975; F. J. Franco 1981). Through the influence of positivism—with its rallying cry of "Civilization or Death!"—Dominicans realized how backward their country really was and intensively debated the causes of its lack of development (González 1987, 11–12; Landolfi 1981, 137). Most of them had a negative vision about the country's situation and its future, therefore, the use of the term *pessimism.* José Ramón López, in his essay "La alimentación y las razas" (Nourishment and the Races), argued that the problems of the Dominican Republic were the result of poor nutrition, which produced new generations that were more decadent than the previous ones ([1896] 1955). Like his upper-class colleagues, López did not consider the Dominican Republic a viable nation. Others, like Federico García Godoy, attributed the political chaos and social decadence of the nation to its mixed ethnic composition. According to García Godoy, who wrote *El derrumbe* (*The Landslide*), the Dominican people were the mixed product of the Spanish lower classes and the savage and superstitious black Africans (F. J. Franco 1981, 88). The preferred solution to these problems was the promotion of immigration. White immigration, it was argued, not only would foster economic development and peace, but would also help "purify" the ethnic composition of the Dominican people (Cassá 1975, 65–66). These racist arguments, though not directly related to antihaitianismo ideology, helped reproduce the prejudices of the Dominican elites. By and large, most of Hostos's disciples used racist arguments in one form or another.

By the late nineteenth century, blacks and dark mulattos still occupied the lower portion of the Dominican social pyramid, in spite of the fact that a black man, Ulises Heureaux, occupied the presidency during the last decade of that century. Heureaux himself was the target of vicious racial insults and personal attacks for his black color and Haitian ancestry.[17] His political opponents would shout or paint slogans like "Down with the Negro!" and "Down with the *mañé!*"[18] (Deive 1976, 90). Even "liberal" thinkers like Eugenio Deschamps called Heureaux a monkey, and Hostos referred to him as "that blackener of Quisqueyanismo,"[19] while Luperón (a black man himself) accused him of being too lax about Haitian infiltration into the Dominican Republic (Hoetink 1982, 189). As these developments have shown, antihaitianismo ideology, even though relations with Haiti had been fairly uneventful for decades, was far from dormant among the Dominican elites. This ideology was often used as a tool that helped the light-skinned elites subjugate and co-opt the dark-skinned Dominican lower classes.

The writings of other important intellectuals of the late nineteenth and early twentieth centuries clearly reflect the anti-Haitian attitudes of the Dominican upper classes. José Gabriel García, Francisco Henríquez y Carvajal, and Américo Lugo, among others, express the general racial prejudices of the time, but with a strong anti-Haitian slant. Dominican literature at the turn of the century is even more prolific regarding anti-Haitian attitudes. Novels, short stories, and poems exalted "Dominican" traits, while denigrating, to the point of making them appear barbaric, Haitian influences. Tulio M. Cestero, Francisco Gregorio Billini, César Nicolás Penson, Federico García Godoy, Francisco Eugenio Moscoso Puello, and Juan Antonio Alix developed a nationalist narrative and poetry that contrasted Dominican Hispanic values with Haiti's African superstitions and customs (Vega 1988, 26–38).

After the assassination of Heureaux by his political opponents in 1899, the Dominican Republic fell back into a vicious circle of *caudillismo,* political instability, and economic indebtedness. The issue of the large foreign debt forced the Dominican government to accept the imposition of a customs receivership in 1907. The agreement gave U.S. agents control over Dominican customhouses in order to ensure the regular payment of the external debt. Still, between 1899 and 1916, the Dominican Republic had eighteen rulers. Political instability, U.S. national security concerns over the Caribbean region, and the U.S. military occupation of Haiti in 1915 eventually led the United States to send marines into the Dominican Republic in 1916. The U.S. military occupation lasted until 1924 (Calder 1984).

Américo Lugo (1870–1952) is the most important Dominican intellectual of the early twentieth century, both for the coherence of his writings and for his strong, patriotic stance against the occupation of the Dominican Republic by U.S. military forces. A disciple of Hostos, Lugo carried on the pessimist legacy of his predecessors by maintaining that the Dominican people did not constitute a nation: "Due to the possession of a too fertile territory under a tropical climate, to the deficiency in nourishment, to the excessive mixture of African blood, to anarchical individualism, and to the lack of culture, the Dominican people have very little political aptitude" ([1916] 1949, 40–41). As seen by his concern about "African blood," Lugo shared the racial prejudices typical of his elite class.[20] Moreover, in his anti-imperialist struggle against the U.S. military occupation, Lugo tried to rally the Dominican people under the old nationalist banner of Hispanic culture. As a bulwark against the Anglo-Saxon culture of the foreign invader, Lugo promoted the "superior" Latin culture of the Dominican people: Spanish language, Catholic religion, and Hispanic traditions (Brea 1985, 48–49). Hispanism, lethargic since Spain's defeat in 1865, was revived by Lugo and his group as a reaction to the sociopolitical and moral crisis provoked by the U.S. military occupation.

Lugo and a whole generation of young Dominican intellectuals had been influenced, in turn, by the publication (in 1900) of the book *Ariel,* by the Uruguayan writer José Enrique Rodó. *Ariel* had a profound impact on Latin American intellectuals. In the Dominican Republic, *arielistas* were characterized by their idealistic, anti-imperialist, and nationalist discourse (Mateo 1993, 58–60). Their exaltation of Hispanic values, though not anti-Haitian per se, was intrinsically racist and paved the road for the anti-Haitian ideological constructions of the Trujillo era (Cassá 1975, 73).

The U.S. military occupation, besides reviving Hispanic values, added a new dimension to antihaitianismo ideology: the presence of a noticeable migrant Haitian population in the Dominican Republic. It was during this period that the large-scale importation of Haitian workers became an established practice. These workers served as cheap labor for the booming Dominican sugar industry—which for the most part was in foreign hands— and for the public works programs of the U.S. military occupation (Castillo 1982, 17–18). The previous importation from the Lesser Antilles of black laborers (known as *cocolos*) had also proven to be more expensive and problematic (because most of them were British subjects). Haitians, on the other hand, were illiterate, worked for very little money, and, since Haiti also was under U.S. military occupation (1915–34), there were practically no legal barriers to their importation. In the view of the Dominican elites, the Dominican people's traditional enemy was now returning, this time not as a conqueror but as a stealthy infiltrator.

Haitian migration added an important element to antihaitianismo ideology. Haitians were no longer the powerful and feared enemies of the past. Haiti had undergone decades of political instability and economic decline during the nineteenth century, and the balance of power in Hispaniola had shifted in favor of the Dominican Republic. Even though Haitians still outnumbered Dominicans, the Dominican leadership no longer feared a Haitian military invasion, given the sorry state of Haiti at the turn of the century. Now Haitians were increasingly stereotyped as poor, illiterate migrants who had to sell their labor for starvation wages, doing slavelike work in a foreign country. Instead of fear, Haitians now provoked contempt among Dominicans, who felt racially and culturally superior (Baud 1996, 131–32; Vega 1988). Still, there were concerns among Dominican elites over the pernicious effect of the Haitian "pacific invasion" on the Dominican people.

The importation of black—and particularly Haitian—workers became a cause of alarm for traditional Dominican elites because it was seen as a threat that undermined their patriarchal power and their aspirations for a racially homogenous society. The newspapers of the time—particularly the *Listín Diario*—are full of complaints about the immigration of black laborers. In 1912, an immigration law was approved in order to curtail black migration. All workers of any race—except Caucasians—needed an immigration permit from the executive branch in order to come to work in the Dominican Republic (Castillo 1978, 44–45). In 1919, U.S. military governor Thomas Snowden issued Executive Order #372, which exerted immigration controls over non-Caucasian immigrants (Castillo 1978, 48).

However, attempts at regulating black migration crashed against the reality of the labor needs of the sugar industry and its powerful influence over the Dominican government. A 1922 report on the Dajabón and Restauración school districts complains about the notorious presence of Haitians in those districts (about 45 percent of the population, according to the report), about their disregard for immigration laws, and about the health problem that they represented (Rodríguez Demorizi 1975, 213–21). Another report from the Santiago school district comments: "However, the constant immigrations of Haitians that establish families in the

Map 2. Haiti and the Dominican Republic

country are increasing the proportion of blacks. This tendency of ethnic degeneration is alarming, as Haitian fertility is proverbial and its population is more numerous than ours. As can be seen, we are facing a national problem of capital importance for the future" (Rodríguez Demorizi 1975, 132). The "Haitian problem" became an important issue of elite debate during the early twentieth century, and the racist, anti-Haitian prejudices of the Dominican elites were as strong and widespread as ever. Now the Dominican nation imagined by its elites seemed to be threatened on two fronts: first, by U.S. imperialism, and second, by (black) Haitian migration. The response of the Dominican elites was vociferous but weak (Baud 1996). Once again, it rested on the fabrication of a mythological Hispanic society with deep roots in the nation's past. There was little, however, that Hispanophile Dominican elites could do at the time, as the country was still under U.S. military occupation.

The withdrawal of the U.S. military forces in 1924 and the election of President Horacio Vásquez did little to alleviate "the Haitian problem." The sugar industry increasingly depended on cheap Haitian labor, at the same time that complaints about the Haitian "pacific invasion" were commonplace (Vega 1988, 22). The high point of the Vásquez administration was the signing of a border treaty with Haiti in 1929, which eventually established the first formal border between Haiti and the Dominican Republic (see map 2). Though hailed as a major event, the treaty failed to stop Haitian migration into the Dominican Republic. The sugar industry needed thousands of cheap laborers every year, and migrants never paid much attention to formal borders. Although official anti-Haitian attitudes were at a low point after the 1929 border treaty, the stage had been set for a confrontation. The coming to power of a ruthless nationalist dictator, General Rafael L. Trujillo, the unfulfilled national aspirations of a generation of Hispanophile elite intellectuals, plus the apparent failure of the 1929 border treaty to curb Haitian migration would lead Haiti and the Dominican Republic to their bloodiest period of confrontation in almost a century: the Trujillo era.

2

Antihaitianismo and State Ideology during the Trujillo Era

One of the many official titles of dictator Rafael L. Trujillo was "Padre de la Patria Nueva" (Father of the New Fatherland), and by most accounts, the Trujillo regime (1930–61) represented a break with the past. The Trujillo era brought profound changes to the Dominican Republic: socially, economically, and even in the development of a new vision of the state and the nation itself.

In their examination of the illusion of nationhood, Etienne Balibar and Immanuel Wallerstein argue: "The formation of the nation thus appears as the fulfillment of a 'project' stretching over centuries, in which there are different stages and moments of coming to self-awareness, which the prejudices of the various historians will portray as more or less decisive . . . but which, in any case, all fit into an identical pattern: that of the self-manifestation of the national personality" (1991, 86). This conceptualization fits the ideological process that took place during the authoritarian regime of Dominican dictator General Trujillo. Besides co-optation and repression, Trujillo employed ideology as a source of political support (Cassá 1982; F. J. Franco 1973; Mateo 1993; Rodríguez de León 1996; Wiarda 1968).

The Trujillista ideology, above all, revered Trujillo as a messianic leader. It also esteemed Hispanic culture and Catholicism as the core of the Dominican nation and attacked communism as a foreign, violent, and atheistic ideology (Cassá 1982). Finally, the Trujillo regime had a strong anti-

Haitian nationalist slant. It concocted the hitherto loose and unorganized ideas of antihaitianismo into a full-fledged ideology that perceived Haitians as inferior beings and enemies of the Dominican nation. Haitians were considered blacks with an Afro-French culture, an alien and pernicious presence in the Dominican Republic. The development of antihaitianismo into a dominant, state-sponsored ideology, and the parallel fabrication of an official nationhood by the Trujillista state, proved to be useful for Trujillo's political survival.

This chapter examines the intellectual component of the anti-Haitian strategy of the Trujillo regime. It discusses the intellectual production of the regime's best minds in order to reveal the inner workings and contradictions of antihaitianismo ideology.

From Friend to Foe

When General Rafael L. Trujillo assumed the presidency of the Dominican Republic in 1930, thus beginning the thirty-one-year dictatorship known as the Trujillo era, relations with Haiti were cordial. The Dominican Republic and Haiti had just signed (in 1929) a border delimitation agreement. Furthermore, Haiti was under U.S. military occupation until 1934, and the United States expressed great interest in solving the problem of the border (Vega 1988, 188). Trujillo was also in the process of consolidating his power and did not want Haiti to be used as a base of operations by anti-Trujillista exiles. Relations between Haiti and the Dominican Republic from 1930 to 1937 were thus essentially "normal." In 1935 and 1936, Presidents Trujillo and Sténio Vincent of Haiti signed additional clauses to the 1929 border treaty, finally establishing a permanent, fixed border between the two countries of Hispaniola. Both leaders visited each other several times, and the press in both countries showered them with praise (Vega 1988).

By 1937, however, Trujillo realized that drawing a legal border had little impact on the way of life of the inhabitants of the borderlands. Haitians—and Haitian-Dominican *fronterizos*—kept crossing into the Dominican Republic to sell goods or to work the land, as they had been doing for decades.[1] The fronterizos spoke Haitian Creole with the same ease as Spanish, and the Haitian gourde circulated freely in the border region (Crassweller 1966, chap. 11). A tour of the border region by Trujillo allowed him to confirm personally these facts of "border life." Trujillo then opted for a radical solution. In October of 1937, Trujillo ordered the assassination of Haitians residing in the Dominican Republic (Cuello 1985; Derby and Turits 1993; Vega 1995). Estimates of the number of dead range from 1,000 to 35,000.[2] Thousands of others, including black Dominicans, escaped into Haiti (Inoa 1993). This repression was Trujillo's draconian way of securing his domains and eliminating what he considered a pernicious influence on the Dominican nation. By physically eliminating the Haitian presence in the borderlands and other parts of the country, Trujillo could begin anew with a "blank slate."[3]

After the 1937 massacre, Trujillo's Haitian policy took a drastic turn. Relations between both countries were strained, and international outrage over the massacre forced Trujillo to lobby for the restoration of his international status. At the national level, Trujillo used the 1937 massacre as the starting point of a grandiose "Dominicanization" policy, designed to secure, develop, and transform the Dominican borderlands into a national showcase. This policy was also aimed at bolstering his personal control over the national territory and building Dominican nationalism into a cultural shield against "foreign" (that is, Haitian) influences.

For this task, Trujillo recruited the services of some of the best intellectuals who still remained in the country and cooperated with the dictator: particularly Manuel A. Peña Batlle and Joaquín Balaguer.[4] These intellectuals created the ideological background to Trujillo's nationalist, anti-Haitian policies. The Trujillo regime and its intellectuals did not invent antihaitianismo; it already was an integral part of Dominican culture. What the Trujillo regime did was to take antihaitianismo to new intellectual heights and convert it into a state-sponsored ideology. The regime's intellectuals transformed popular anti-Haitian prejudices, and the elite's Hispanophile ideas, into a complex, yet historically flawed, dominant ideology. Additionally, the regime launched a massive propaganda program designed to bolster its support by promoting anti-Haitian nationalism. These efforts reached their peak during the late 1930s and early 1940s, when relations with Haiti were at a low point (Vega 1994a). In the 1950s, by contrast, the Trujillo regime maintained good relations with Haiti, and antihaitianismo ideology practically disappeared from the official discourse—though it remained entrenched in most practices and institutions.

A State-sponsored Anti-Haitian Ideology

After the 1937 massacre, the regime's main ideological strategy was to foster anti-Haitian nationalism, which had remained dormant given Trujillo's good relations with Vincent. First, the strategy involved the creation of a myth to justify the horrendous 1937 massacre. And second, Trujillo encouraged the development of a nationalist, anti-Haitian state ideology, designed to establish a clear and permanent separation between Haiti and the Dominican Republic in the minds of the Dominican people and thus build loyalty to his regime.

Andrés L. Mateo (1993) argues that the uniqueness of the Trujillo regime lay in its use of myths and deception as political tools, while Roberto Cassá emphasizes "the deliberate, organic and elementary purpose of institutional deception" (1982, 60). To justify the 1937 massacre, Trujillo's ideologues created the myth of peace and national security. Accordingly, only Trujillo's use of extreme measures saved the Dominican Republic from "the Haitian danger." If the border was still intact, it was only thanks to Trujillo (Mateo 1993, 112–16). Furthermore, official references to the 1937 massacre were absent. No documentation with direct references to the massacre—before, during, or after it—has been found in Dominican archives (Cuello 1985). It was as if it never happened. And for many Dominicans, misinformed by Trujillo's propaganda machine, it never did.

The ideology of antihaitianismo, as promoted during the Trujillo era, operated on simple principles: Haitians were an inferior people, the pure descendants of black African slaves who were illiterate, malnourished, disease-ridden, and believed in voodoo; Dominicans, on the other hand, were portrayed as the proud descendants of the Catholic Spanish conquistadores and the brave Taíno Indians (Sagás 1993). This distorted vision of Dominican society led to a rejection of black elements in Dominican culture in favor of a state-promoted Hispanic cultural heritage.[5] Haiti was again portrayed as the perennial enemy of the Dominican people, bent on taking over the east, this time using massive immigration. Based on these principles, Trujillo's ideologues developed a state-sponsored dominant ideology.

Manuel A. Peña Batlle

In this Trujillista ideological project, the figure of Manuel Arturo Peña Batlle (1902–54) towered well above all the other intellectuals of the Trujillo regime for his scholarship, coherence, and impact on the policy-making process. According to historian Emilio Rodríguez Demorizi, Peña Batlle was "the brightest and most decided interpreter of Trujillo's political ideas" (González 1994, 23).

Peña Batlle's thought had been influenced by the liberal tradition of Eugenio María de Hostos and Américo Lugo, two of the brightest minds of their time. He initially opposed the Trujillo regime but by 1935 was working for the government. He actively participated in the border delimitation process and held several government positions, such as ambassador, adviser, secretary of state of foreign relations, and secretary of state of interior and police. Peña Batlle also was an accomplished historian; he wrote several historical works ([1946] 1988, 1951, 1952, 1954a), in which he presented his ideas on the origins and essence of the Dominican nation.

Peña Batlle's main preoccupation—bordering on an obsession—was the duality of the island of Hispaniola, which he considered detrimental to the interests of the Dominican Republic. For him, the presence of Haiti—and before it the French colony of Saint-Domingue—had had serious and pernicious consequences for Dominican development since colonial times. Peña Batlle idealized the Spanish colony of Santo Domingo as a society without racial or class-based conflicts, where even slavery was benign. Slaves are usually mentioned in his writings only in relation to Haiti, while their role in Spanish Santo Domingo is minimized or ignored altogether (González 1994, 43).

Haiti, in contrast, is considered a nation created as the result of a bloody racial conflict. According to Peña Batlle, this irreconcilable duality sparked the separatist movement that led to Dominican independence in 1844. Peña Batlle stressed that "the separation from Haiti was a reactive movement, in defense of Hispanic culture" (San Miguel 1992, 101–3). From then on, the history of the Dominican Republic is depicted by Peña Batlle as shaped by the defense of its culture and territory from Haitian aggression.

In his writings, Peña Batlle also embarked on the task of distorting Haitian-Dominican history so as to portray Haitians as hostile foreigners, culturally and racially inferior to the Dominican people. In his famous address to the border town of Elías Piña (on 16 November 1942), "El sentido de una política" (A Policy's Sense), Peña Batlle clearly displays the state's official line on Haitian migration:

There is no feeling of humanity, nor political reason, nor any circumstantial convenience that can force us to look indifferently at the Haitian penetration. That type is frankly undesirable. Of pure African race, he cannot represent for us any ethnic incentive. Not well nourished and worse dressed, he is weak, though very prolific due to his low living conditions. For that same reason, the Haitian that enters [our country] lives afflicted by numerous and capital vices and is necessarily affected by diseases and physiological deficiencies which are endemic at the lowest levels of that society. (1954b, 67–68)

Little can be added to Peña Batlle's statement. The Trujillo regime and its anti-Haitian ideology—as expressed by Peña Batlle—rejected Haitian migration on racial, human, and even sanitary grounds.

In his "Carta al Doctor Mañach," Peña Batlle goes a step farther. He defends Trujillo's Haitian policy and places the Haitian-Dominican conflict in a distorted historical perspective. According to Peña Batlle, the conflict between Haitians and Dominicans in his time was just the modern version of the old conflict between the invading French buccaneers and the Spanish colonial authorities. Thus Peña Batlle established a (flimsy) historical bond between the Haitian migrant of the twentieth century and the French invaders of the past. Just like the French buccaneers of Tortuga Island, the Haitian migrants of Peña Batlle's time were portrayed as hostile foreign invaders who coveted the whole island of Hispaniola. Based on these arguments, he went on to justify Trujillo's authoritarian methods:

In the Dominican Republic there should not be, there cannot be, a government so uninterested in the use of force that it turns itself, as it has happened many times, into an agent of Haitian expansionism. Democracy, as understood and exercised in some countries, is a luxury that we cannot afford. When will you Cubans, our dearest neighbors, understand that truth? Know this well, Minister, as soon as the Haitians stop fearing us, they will bite us: silently, quietly, without you or anyone knowing about it. (1954b, 96)

Peña Batlle here (re)employs an old argument in Dominican political thought: that the Dominican Republic is a backward country that cannot be governed the way developed countries are.

Since the nineteenth century, Dominican leaders have argued that democracy cannot flourish in an unruly country like the Dominican Republic. A strongman, a caudillo, is needed (Avelino 1966). According to Peña Batlle, given the grave danger that Haiti represented, authoritarian measures were justified. Here Peña Batlle removed the democratic facade that adulatory writers had imposed on the Trujillo regime and instead justified it on historical grounds. If the Dominican Republic was not a democratic country, it was Haiti's fault, according to this line of reasoning. If the Dominican Republic had a stern government, it was because only a strongman could protect the country's integrity. Trujillo, authoritarian as he may have been, was the savior of the Dominican nation. As Peña Batlle made it explicitly clear to Mañach, a Cuban minister who had published an article on Haiti and the Dominican Republic: "The methods of discipline, exaggerated if you want, are essential in the life of the Dominican people" (1954b, 97).

Manuel A. Peña Batlle represented the zenith of antihaitianismo ideology. No other intellectual during the Trujillo era produced a more coherent and scholarly interpretation of the regime's official ideology. Most of those that followed him simply repeated his basic arguments, though with less coherence and scholarship.

Joaquín Balaguer

Just as Peña Batlle defended Trujillo's actions from a historical perspective, Joaquín Balaguer (1906-) served as one of the regime's most efficient and outspoken apologists (Rodríguez de León 1996). At the time of the 1937 massacre, Balaguer—then just thirty-one years old—worked as interim chancellor (or undersecretary of state of foreign relations). He was entrusted with the diplomatic defense of the Trujillo regime in the international arena, and with the negotiations that took place with the Haitian government after the massacre. As minister to Colombia in 1945, Balaguer published two open letters in the newspaper *El Tiempo,* in which he portrayed the 1937 massacre as merely a series of incidents between Dominican peasants and Haitian cattle rustlers. He also defended the Trujillo regime as the savior of the Dominican nation, a nation "condemned to disappear absorbed by Haiti, a more prolific and homogenous race than ours" (Cuello 1985, 503–8).

In *La realidad dominicana,*[6] considered one of the most brilliant apologies of the Trujillo regime, Balaguer justifies Trujillo's anti-Haitian policy as part of the natural and inalienable right of the Dominican people to defend their culture and way of life:

> There is, therefore, no reason either of justice or of humanity, which can prevail against the right of the Dominican people to exist as a Spanish country and as a Christian community. (1947, 123)

> The race problem is, therefore, the principal problem of the Dominican Republic. But if the racial problem is of incalculable importance to all countries, in Santo Domingo the matter takes on immense proportions, as upon it depends, after a fashion, the very existence of the nationality that has for over a century been struggling against a more prolific race. (1947, 124–25)

Notice how Balaguer makes indistinct use of the terms *race* and *nationality,* so as to pretend that Haitians and Dominicans belonged not only to different nations but also to completely different races. As he sees it, these are "two antagonistic races, one of Spanish origin, and the other Ethiopian" (Balaguer 1947, 115). Because of its racial makeup, Balaguer considers Haitian society to be inferior and uncivilized:

> Incest and other practices no less barbaric and antagonistic to the Christian institution of the family are common among the lower classes of the population of Haiti and give testimony of its appalling moral deformities. (1947, 94)

> The Negro who emigrates to Santo Domingo is a being marked by horrible physical defects. (1947, 102)

> The Haitian immigrant has also been a generator of sloth in Santo Domingo. The Ethiopian race is indolent by nature and applies no special efforts to anything useful unless it is forced to obtain its subsistence by that means. (1947, 104)

These racist arguments were used by Balaguer to justify the necessity of preserving the integrity of the Dominican nation against Haitian penetration.

Like Peña Batlle, Balaguer also distorted Dominican history to further his cause. In *La realidad dominicana,* Balaguer portrays Santo Domingo as a colony made of European families that became filled with African slaves as a result of the 1795 cession to France (1947, 109). In the same work, he also accuses Haiti of wishing to conquer the whole island, either through military invasions (up to 1856) or the usurpation of Dominican territory (since 1861) (1947, 85). Again, Balaguer considers Trujillo the savior of the Dominican Republic by, first, establishing a fixed border, and second, eliminating all traces of the Haitian presence in the borderlands. Some of these tasks, like the elimination of Haitian pillage in the borderlands, he adds, could not "be accomplished easily and with no bloodshed," a veiled reference to the 1937 incidents (1947, 90).

Balaguer's antihaitianismo clearly lacks the historical coherence of Peña Batlle's arguments. His arguments are based on outdated and unfounded theories of racial inferiority, some of them dating back to the nineteenth century. Furthermore, his portrayal of Dominican history is romantic at best, and his "historical" examples are weak. However, Balaguer's strongest contribution to antihaitianismo ideology was in his role as statesman. During the Trujillo era, he occupied several important government posts, including the presidency, from which he defended and furthered the policies of the Trujillo regime.

Other Ideologues

Remarks, critiques, or verbal attacks against the official ideology of anti-haitianismo were swiftly and systematically dealt with by Trujillo's ideologues. For example, the publication in 1953 of Jean Price-Mars's *La República de Haití y la República Dominicana,*[7] an examination of Haitian-Dominican relations with a clear *noiriste* slant, provoked a barrage of vicious literary attacks against the book and its author. Sócrates Nolasco and Angel S. del Rosario Pérez, two intellectuals at the regime's service, wrote bitter criticisms of Price-Mars's work.

In a provocative book titled *La exterminación añorada,* Angel Rosario Pérez (1957) takes on Price-Mars. In this mammoth work (402 pages, divided into thirty-eight chapters), he levies one charge after another against Price-Mars. He accuses Price-Mars of being a racist, of distorting historical facts to his advantage, and even of wishing that the Dominican people had been exterminated by the Haitian armies in the early nineteenth century. In the process, Rosario Pérez does some historical distorting of his own, such as claiming that African slaves were only brought into Santo Domingo between 1510 and 1550, and that those slaves were of peaceful coastal extraction. Slaves brought into Saint-Domingue were, on the other hand, mostly ferocious savages, including many sorcerers and cannibals (Rosario Pérez 1957, 28–29). He then justifies slavery as "the exploitation of masses that, anyway, were being devoured in Africa by their own kind" (1957, 90). In his view, Price-Mars is a "Dessalinian thinker" (a reference to the Haitian leader who invaded Santo Domingo in 1805), and the Dominican people are a collective "goat without horns" (1957, 381).[8] Haitians, according to Rosario Pérez, think about expanding only at the Dominican Republic's expense. For that reason—and not surprisingly—"only in the identification with Trujillo's ideas will the future Dominican generations find their survival" (Rosario Pérez 1957, 402).

In his 1955 book, Sócrates Nolasco also attacks Price-Mars's work, but his tone is more subtle. While recognizing Price-Mars's achievements and scholarship, he criticizes the author's noiriste bias and his historical fallacies. In the conclusion, as was customary, Nolasco is obliged to pay homage to Trujillo, and he participates in the common myth of Haitian expansionist designs against the Dominican Republic. Haitians, according to him, "have only stopped at the sight of multiple colonies and schools on the frontier, and, watchful, Trujillo's army on the border line convened in 1935" (1955, 46). Once again, Trujillo appears as the savior of the Dominican nation.

With the publication of *El caso dominico-haitiano (Separata)* in 1958, Carlos Augusto Sánchez y Sánchez, professor of law at the Universidad de Santo Domingo, joined the debate about Price-Mars's book. Sánchez y Sánchez had proposed a solution to Haiti's overpopulation problem that infuriated Price-Mars: the movement of Haiti's excess population to another location under an international mandate directed by the Haitian government (Sánchez y Sánchez 1958, 76–78). In his book, Sánchez y Sánchez defends this proposal by arguing that Haiti's overpopulation represents a danger to the Dominican Republic, its only neighbor. Haiti would naturally dump its excess population on the Dominican Republic, a nation with different racial and cultural characteristics. Sánchez y Sánchez then repeats the same arguments of Peña Batlle and Balaguer about the racial and cultural differences between Haiti and the Dominican Republic: Haiti is a black nation with an Afro-French culture, whereas the Dominican Republic is a mulatto country with a Hispanic-Catholic culture. He even argues that Dominicans are the rightful heirs of the island, because traces of Indian blood can still be found in the Dominican people (1958, 43–46). Finally, he accuses Price-Mars of reverse discrimination, that is, of discriminating against whites, and points out that—unlike in Haiti—there is no racial discrimination in the Dominican Republic. In the Dominican Republic blacks have acquired a Western culture and think like white Spaniards, while black Haitians from the lower classes think like Africans (Sánchez y Sánchez 1958, 27).

Finally, historian Emilio Rodríguez Demorizi produced a number of works that were instrumental in creating an interpretation of Haitian-Dominican history more in accord with the tenets of antihaitianismo ideology, and in providing the documentation for such endeavors. A particular brand of historical production flourished during the Trujillo era, as Cassá points out: "The despot himself acted as sponsor of the historiographic production destined to justify his presence, to glorify the colonial past, to 'demonstrate' the Hispanic character of the Dominican people, to highlight the more negative aspects of the history of the past, as was the case during the pro-Santana campaign, and, notably, to detract the Haitian nation and portray it as a permanent and irreducible enemy" (1975, 79). As the most prolific historian of the Trujillo era, Rodríguez Demorizi produced works that were trendsetters in this regard. Certainly, his scholarship was impressive: Rodríguez Demorizi wrote or compiled hundreds of books and articles on Dominican history and culture. His position as one of the regime's top historians gave him unlimited access to national and even foreign archives. For example, his compilations of documents are still basic reference sources for the study of Dominican history and are even used by leftist and revisionist historians.

As an intellectual at the regime's service, however, Rodríguez Demorizi's scholarship was also tainted with the official anti-Haitian bias of the dictatorship. His valuable compilations of documents were often preceded by long introductions or extensively annotated with footnotes that reflected his (and the regime's) anti-Haitian views. For example, his position on Haitian migration to the Dominican Republic cannot be clearer: "This last class of immigrants is of the worst kind. Negroes in its totality, almost naked, illiterate, usually famished and sick, nomad tribes without anything, dark caravans that brought with them misery, superstitions, amorality, voodoo, Africanization" (1955a, 46). His racial ideas paralleled those of Peña Batlle and Balaguer, and like them, he portrayed Dominican history as the never-ending struggle of a Catholic and Hispanic nation to avoid being forcefully absorbed by its more densely populated Afro-French neighbor, which held "vain and sinister dreams of political indivisibility of the island to the detriment of its legitimate masters" (1971, 93). In this vein, he published several works to document the "traumatic" cession of Santo Domingo to France in 1795, the Haitian invasions of the eastern part of the island, and the Haitian-Dominican wars of the 1840s and 1850s (1955a, 1955b, 1957, 1958).

Rodríguez Demorizi also participated in the debate generated by the publication of Jean Price-Mars's book. In his rebuttal, he accuses Price-Mars of distorting historical facts, of pretending that the differences between Haitians and Dominicans are of grade and not of kind, of having a superiority complex, and of portraying Haitian history as beginning in 1492, with Columbus's arrival, when it actually began around 1650, when the first buccaneers established themselves in Tortuga island (1955a, 48–68).

Trujillo's intellectuals provided the regime with the ideological underpinning that his authoritarian, sultanistic rule needed. But antihaitianismo, as an important component of the regime's ideology, did not operate in a political vacuum. It was supported by authoritarian measures, policies, and institutions. The Trujillo regime implemented state policies in which the spread of antihaitianismo ideology became a major priority, as part of an orchestrated plan to subjugate and control the Dominican people. The Trujillista intellectuals provided the ideas; the Trujillo regime provided the means to this end.

3

Antihaitianismo as a Political Tool for Trujillo

Trujillo's long dictatorship represented the turn of the tide in Haitian-Dominican relations. The Trujillo era witnessed the rise of the Dominican Republic as the main power in the island. No longer did the Dominican Republic have to search for a foreign protector in order to keep Haiti at bay. To the contrary, it was now Haiti that had to fear the growing power of the Dominican Republic. The delimitation of the border, the 1937 massacre, and the border region settlement program helped "clean" the borderlands of Haitian influences and integrated the region into the national mainstream. Furthermore, Trujillo's immigration policies and imposed "peace" in the countryside enabled the Dominican people to achieve finally the necessary population growth rates to start catching up to Haiti's larger population. Hefty budget allocations of over 20 percent of the national budget transformed the Dominican armed forces into one of the better armed in Latin America (Sagás 1988, 25), capable of easily defeating the Haitian army.

Through a combination of bribery and intimidation, Trujillo also influenced Haitian politics. He bribed and kept on his personal payroll dozens of Haitian politicians, administrators, ambassadors, and military officers. Even some Haitian presidents (in particular Élie Lescot) were in Trujillo's payroll since the beginning of their political careers (Crassweller 1966, chap. 11; Delince 1993, 273–74). Trujillo's agents also roamed Haiti's territory carrying out his orders and keeping at bay Dominican exiles who tried to use Haiti as a base of operations against the Trujillo regime (Vega 1988). This constant infringement of Haitian sovereignty was just another of Trujillo's tactics to exert control and to demonstrate to Haitians and Dominicans alike who was the "boss" in Hispaniola.[1] These actions represented a new style in Haitian-Dominican relations, a style characterized by the preeminence of the Dominican Republic and the active meddling of its leader in Haitian affairs. This manipulative style was unique to Trujillo and has not been repeated with subsequent leaders.

Trujillo also supported antihaitianismo ideology with strong actions at the national level. These authoritarian measures were part of a multifaceted strategy to consolidate and maintain absolute power. Antihaitianismo ideology, with its strong nationalist content, was perfect for these purposes. This chapter reviews the measures and programs implemented by the Trujillo regime to spread the ideas of antihaitianismo among the Dominican people in what essentially became a national brainwashing effort. The chapter also explores how this ideology was used to divide and disorient the subordinate classes.

Several institutions were employed to propagate and institutionalize antihaitianismo as a state ideology: the Catholic Church, the state machinery, and Trujillo's Partido Dominicano. All three of them converged after 1937 on the regime's newest grandiose project: the Dominicanization of the borderlands.

Dominicanization of the Border Region

After the 1937 massacre, the Trujillo regime took steps to thoroughly Dominicanize the border region. This project was not a new idea among Dominican leaders; president Horacio Vásquez (1924–30) had built several towns in the borderlands, but those were only tentative steps. Trujillo himself continued Vásquez's policies, but they were largely ineffective in stopping Haitian migration into the Dominican Republic. After the drastic "cleansing" of the border region in 1937, the Trujillo regime sought to erect a human shield against Haitian migration; "an absolutely impassable social, ethnic, economic, and religious fence" (Peña Batlle 1954b, 63). In the words of three regime intellectuals (Emilio Rodríguez Demorizi, Héctor Incháustegui Cabral, and Ramón Marrero Aristy): "We, who cannot split the island in two, . . . have to build in the border with our own entrails the wall of social, economic, and political interests that will safeguard us from the evil that all the civilized nations of the world keep within bounds" (*Para la historia dos cartas* 1943, 12). Plans were drawn in which the border region would be transformed into a national showcase.

The government established several agricultural colonies on the border region in an attempt to increase both the population and agricultural production of the region. By 1952, there were seventeen border colonies with a total population of 19,276. Many of these colonists, including common prisoners, were forcefully relocated to the border region (Box and de la Rive Box-Lasocki 1989, 56–57). The regime also built military outposts that increased the state's presence in the region and, as a result, Trujillo's control over the national territory.

The Dominicanization of the border region, however, was a greater success on paper than in reality. The border region remained isolated from the national mainstream, with little influence on the country's economy. But the state's propaganda machine offered a different picture, boasting about its cosmetic achievements. Several works were written about the deplorable conditions of the region and how things drastically improved after the Dominicanization program was implemented (Hernández Franco 1943; Herraiz 1957; R. E. Jiménez 1953; Machado Báez 1955; Peñolguín 1940). In these laudatory works, the border region was invariably described as a poor and depopulated no-man's-land, where everyone spoke Creole, and where the absence of the state made it difficult to distinguish Dominicans from Haitians. Trujillo then changed everything. Living conditions in the border region under the Trujillo regime were described in superlative terms. The new border towns had government buildings, private dwellings, hospitals, hotels, electricity, recreation rooms, asylums, Catholic schools, maternity homes, Catholic churches, priest houses, and other services, according to these works (Herraiz 1957, 416).[2]

The Dominicanization of the border region provides a good example of the practical application of antihaitianismo ideology. The Trujillo regime combined official propaganda with authoritarian measures and construction projects to make the border region an impenetrable human barrier. The state sought not only to recover its authority over territories that had been considered "lost" to Haiti, but also to eradicate all forms of Haitian presence and influence in these regions. An examination of three institutions will show how they worked closely to disseminate antihaitianismo ideology and eradicate Haitian influences not only in the border region but throughout the nation as well.

The Catholic Church

The pro-Hispanic antihaitianismo ideology established a close connection with the Catholic Church, for Catholicism supposedly was one of the main characteristics of Dominican culture. As the first Spanish colony in the New World, Santo Domingo could claim the primacy of Hispanic culture and Christian values, according to the regime's ideologues (Sáez 1988, 92). Haitians, on the other hand, were portrayed as followers of the African rites commonly known as voodoo, regardless of the popularity of the Catholic religion in Haiti. Catholicism was also seen as a barrier against the spread of communism—labeled as an atheist ideology by the regime. Finally, the Catholic Church, protected and heavily subsidized by the Trujillista state, legitimized Trujillo's rule and called upon its followers to accept his mandate (Cassá 1982, 83). Catholic priests stressed the Hispanic and Catholic character of the Dominican people in their sermons, thus helping reproduce antihaitianismo ideology. This Hispanic-Catholic connection was reinforced by Spanish priests of clear fascist orientation who held great influence over the lower classes, particularly among the peasantry. The Church, through the use of brainwashing techniques such as "spiritual retreats" (two- or three-day religious meetings held in total or partial isolation), instilled among its followers fear of God, conservative values, and respect for the authorities. Government officials, military officers, and intellectuals were periodically forced to participate in these retreats, where their loyalty was tested and renewed (Cordero Michel 1975, 42). On 16 June 1954, Church-state cooperation reached its peak with the signing of a concordat (in Rome) with the Vatican, an event which Trujillo personally attended (Rodríguez de León 1996, 188–92). Both in practical and intellectual terms, Trujillo established a close connection between Church and state that lasted well until late in the Trujillo era.

One of the most important projects undertaken by the Catholic Church and the regime was the "border missions" program, designed to spread the Christian faith among the inhabitants of the borderlands. Until then, it was lamented, these people had been under the pernicious influence of Haitian rites. In August of 1936, Trujillo authorized the Jesuit order to do mission-ary work in the northern border province of Dajabón, with the support of the state. The Jesuits, with their renowned tenacity, soon exercised great influence over the inhabitants of the border region, helping to create the "cultural wall" requested by the regime's intellectuals.

The Jesuits were present in the region during the 1937 massacre, yet none of them made any mention of the killings. A memoir on the border missions, written by Father Antonio López de Santa Anna, draws a picture of the region's inhabitants that seems taken from the writings of Trujillo's ideologues: "Among the inhabitants the Indian race predominates, though not in a pure form; the African race exists, though not as much, mixed in the majority of cases with the Indian or the white race. . . . there are also numerous white families of undisputed Spanish ancestry" (1958, 25). This astounding description asserted that most borderland Dominicans were not mulattos but the descendants of Indians! To be even more specific, López de Santa Anna affirmed that Indians could be differentiated from blacks by their "greater facial angle, Caucasianlike cranium, straight and abundant hair, delicate hands, small teeth, and less height and muscular development than Africans" (1958, 26–27). It is difficult to find a bolder and more prejudiced opinion (and so much in accord with antihaitianismo ideology), even among some of the regime's intellectuals.

The Partido Dominicano

No institution played a larger role in the propaganda efforts of the Trujillo regime than the Partido Dominicano (PD). The PD was officially estab-lished in 1931 and was the only legal party in the Dominican Republic during most of the Trujillo era.[3] The PD became Trujillo's greatest base of support after the armed forces. As part of its mission, the PD propagated antihaitianismo ideology throughout the country. With the help of the PD, the regime's anti-Haitian, pro-Hispanic, and Catholic ideology reached thousands of Dominicans of all social strata. Trujillo himself proclaimed, "The Party has been, by the unavoidable claim of our social circumstances, an agent of civilization" (1955, 30). According to Oviedo (1986), the PD was a major agent of political socialization and a fundamental mediator in the relationship between urban and rural areas. Using the mass media, its control over unions and associations, and public appearances scheduled by intellectuals and party leaders, the PD reached even the most remote corner of the national territory. The PD annually held thousands of meetings, rallies, and marches—2,976 public acts in 1940 alone (Oviedo 1986, 242). It was difficult for any Dominican citizen not to fall under the influence of the PD, as most adults were required to be members of the party.[4] It is estimated that between 3.5 to 4 million Dominicans attended the party's events every year, making of the PD a "machine of permanent psychological action" (Cordero Michel 1975, 38–39).

The PD also played an active and important role in the Dominicanization of the border region. The fifth article of its Declaration of Principles read, "The Party declares that the maintenance of social, political, and economic dominicanidad in the border region is an unavoidable patriotic duty" (Penson 1959, 28). Following this line, the PD constructed houses, presented movies and documentaries, established libraries, and organized thousands of cultural and political meetings in the border region (Penson 1959, 29). Through these efforts, the PD sought to reaffirm Dominican nationalism in the region closest to Haiti, and to strengthen popular support for the Trujillo regime. In short, the PD was one of the main promoters of antihaitianismo ideology during the Trujillo era, particularly in the border region.

The State Machinery

Finally, the state machinery was the other main promoter of antihaitianismo ideology. The Trujillo regime used all the resources and institutions at its disposal in order to gain the minds and hearts of the Dominican people. Dominicans were socialized to think and act as a sole entity with a single purpose: to passively accept the authority of General Trujillo.

One of the regime's first priorities was to shape the future generations. With that in mind, the Trujillo regime paid particular attention to education, which became just another instrument of political domination over the masses. Law 2909 declared that "the content of the education provided by Dominican schools will be based on the principles of Christian civilization and Hispanic tradition that are fundamental in the formation of our historical physiognomy" (Congreso Nacional de la República Dominicana 1951, 3). According to José R. Cordero Michel (1975), the orientation of education was antidemocratic and antiscientific, and based on chauvinistic nationalism, racism, irrational clericalism, and the cult of Trujillo's personality. Furthermore, students were bombarded with nationalist propaganda and taught to hate Haiti and despise blacks (Cordero Michel 1975, 93–94). This educational propaganda not only inflamed national resentment against Haiti but also served to justify the 1937 massacre, the maintenance of a large army, and the exploitation of the black masses. History books were full of distortions, exaggerations, and outright falsifications. A well-illustrated, popular history textbook portrayed Haitians as apelike, while Dominicans were drawn to look like Spaniards (Estella and Alloza [1944] 1986). The book also emphasized the gallant suffering of the Dominican people during the Haitian occupation (1822–44) and their brave actions against the Haitian armies during the independence wars.

Education in the border region was particularly important, due to its proximity to Haiti. Schools in the borderland had an additional educational mission: to act as preservers of language, customs, and patriotic sentiments (P. A. Franco 1940, 3). The educational program included instruction on the national symbols, the national anthem, and the forefathers of the Dominican Republic. History and geography were emphasized, and the border schools were named after Dominican patriots like Duarte, Mella, Sánchez, Luperón, and, of course, Rafael L. Trujillo ("Con hondo sentido" 1938). By 1955, there were 251 schools in the border region, with 20,552 students, according to official sources. In addition, the position of border cultural agent was created, in order to carry out geographic, historical, and civic propaganda in the region (Machado Báez 1955, 232–34). The state spared no resources to fit the new Dominican generations into the mold of the Trujillo regime.

The Trujillista state also made use of other institutions in order to propagate antihaitianismo ideology. The Trujillo regime paid particular attention to the countryside because most of the Dominican population lived in the rural areas. In a handbook for *alcaldes pedáneos* (rural mayors),[5] Trujillo instructed them to watch out for "Haitianizing influences whose consequences will always be extremely fatal for Dominican society" (Ginebra 1940, 8). Law 391 imposed jail terms, fines, and deportation (when appropriate) for those found practicing "voudou" or "*luá*" (voodoo dancing). Moreover, objects used in those rites were to be confiscated and destroyed (Congreso Nacional de la República Dominicana 1943). These measures were aimed at further curbing any Haitian (or black) influences, and at legitimizing and institutionalizing antihaitianismo by giving it the full support of the judicial system and the state bureaucracy. In this particular case, popular Dominican religious practices of Afro-Caribbean origin were deemed anti-Hispanic, falsely linked to Haiti, and thus forbidden by the regime.

The antihaitianismo ideology of the Trujillo regime also influenced literary production. In the literature of the Trujillo era, Haitians were portrayed as inferior beings: resentful, pernicious, and cowardly (A. Despradel 1975). Short stories and novels were published by the regime to describe the problem of Haitian migration to the Dominican Republic. In *Compay Chano* (Román 1949), for example, the two main characters struggle against the depredations of Haitian cattle rustlers, an epic battle between Dominican civilization and Haitian barbarism. Finally, the pacification of the border is achieved with the "expulsion" (a reference to the 1937 massacre) of Haitian migrants (Mateo 1993, 200–202).

The use—and exploitation—of Haitian labor in the then U.S.-owned sugar industry is presented in the novel *Over,* a work of social criticism, by Ramón Marrero Aristy (1939). Regarding Haitian-Dominican relations, the novel clearly portrays the anti-Haitian prejudices of Dominican sugar workers but places the blame on the foreigners who owned the sugar industry and perpetuated the system of exploitation, thus relieving Trujillo of any guilt. However, the novel also contains veiled criticisms of the status quo and ideas that were not in line with the Trujillo regime's official discourse (Sommer 1983, chap. 4). In *Over,* Marrero Aristy certainly threads a dangerous path between general social criticism and treason to the Trujillo regime. As a result, *Over* was only briefly used by the regime's propagandists to fuel their own version of Dominican nationalism. Eventually, Marrero Aristy's "blunders" led to his assassination in 1959.

A favorite theme of the regime's apologists was the influence of voodoo and other Haitian practices (Coradín 1940; González Herrera 1943; Peñolguín 1940; Sanz Lajara 1949), as well as the bloody history and politics of Haiti (Viau 1955). With suggestive names such as *Vodú* and *Negros, mulatos, blancos o sangre, nada más que sangre* (Blacks, Mulattos, Whites or Blood, Nothing but Blood), this literary production deformed Haitian-Dominican reality and was used to justify Trujillo's authority as the guardian of the Dominican nation. For example, González Herrera's *Trementina, clerén y bongó* and Sanz Lajara's *Caonex* defend Trujillo's authoritarian rule as the only option in the face of Haiti's intentions to conquer the island. If not for a strongman like Trujillo, they argue, Haiti by now would have "absorbed" the Dominican nation (Di Pietro 1996, 28–33).

Not even popular music was spared from the pernicious influence of the state's propaganda machinery. Trujillo—due to his lower-class origins—was an ardent fan of merengue music. He promoted merengue to the status of a national dance and used it to politicize the lower classes, particularly the peasantry (Austerlitz 1997, chap. 4). Merengue, by its popular appeal and capacity to disseminate political slogans, is considered one of the most effective propaganda tools of the Trujillo regime (Jorge 1982, 79). Merengues would sing praises to Trujillo's figure, to his great achievements, and to his invincibility. Merengue was also portrayed as the national soul of the Dominican people, another element that differentiated Dominicans from Haitians. Some merengues had nationalist overtones, in accord with the anti-Haitian, Hispanic, Catholic, and anticommunist ideology of the Trujillo regime:

Es nuestra patria cristiana
y por tanto trujillista
que reconoce a Trujillo
líder anticomunista

Our nation is Christian
and thus Trujillista
it recognizes Trujillo
anti-Communist leader.

(Tejada 1978, 33)

Almost five hundred songs were written to praise the dictator. In addition, the regime sponsored musical and folkloric research that stressed the Hispanic roots of Dominican music, while minimizing its African and Haitian influences (Jorge 1982, 84). Besides promoting nationalism, musical compositions praised the Indian past of the Dominican people. Indigenismo, which had been an important trend in Dominican literature during the late nineteenth century, now moved to the musical arena under the auspices of the state.

Class, Race, and Political Subordination

There has always been an intrinsic correlation between class and race in the Dominican Republic, as is the case throughout Latin America. Even though the Dominican people are overwhelmingly mulatto, the upper classes are mostly light-skinned, while the lower classes tend to be dark-skinned.[6] The changes brought about by the lengthy Trujillo regime and the economic modernization of the country during the twentieth century did little to radically change that fact.

When Trujillo became president in 1930, Dominican society was essentially divided in two classes: *gente de primera* (upper-class citizens) and *gente de segunda* (the rest of the population, the masses). Trujillo himself was de segunda and, as a result, was blackballed by the social elites for years. Trujillo never forgot that rejection, and during his dictatorship he tried to break the power of the traditional elites and even humiliate some of them (Crassweller 1966). He also promoted de segunda supporters by giving them high-ranking positions in the army and the state's bureaucracy, which translated into opportunities for their social advancement and personal enrichment. Still, Trujillo needed the acquiescence—or complicity—of the traditional upper classes to maintain power and develop the country's economy. So, at the end of his regime, the only noticeable changes in the social structure of the Dominican Republic were the addition of a layer of newly rich individuals (by their close association with the regime) to the traditional Dominican upper classes, and the expansion of a salaried middle class as a result of economic development and the growth of the state (E. Betances 1995, 103–10).

Race was a central concern of the Trujillo regime. In its permanent struggle for legitimation and control, the Trujillista state often employed it as a recourse. As seen in the previous chapter, race came to be defined by the Trujillo regime not necessarily in terms of color but also in terms of national identity and culture. Race and nationality were artificially confused by the state-sponsored ideology of antihaitianismo, which saw threats to the nation and its culture as coming not only from Haiti (the external, foreign enemy) but also from the black population in the Dominican Republic. References were made by the Trujillista intellectuals to the "Africanization" of the country and the "Ethiopian" hordes of Haitian immigrants.

"Blackness" became the ultimate danger to the paradisiacal Dominican Republic that the Trujillo regime envisioned, and it represented the "interiorization" of the threat. This last aspect of antihaitianismo ideology also helped create the justifications and authoritarian mechanisms for the exploitation of the popular sectors (mostly dark-skinned).

According to Cassá (1975, 77), antihaitianismo has been (to this day) an alienating mechanism and an obstacle to the development of a truly popular and national conscience. Moreover, antihaitianismo ideology consolidated and validated existing social differences and forms of exploitation. For Dominicans, the exploitation of blacks by "whites," which had gone on for so long, became an immutable fact of life, part of nature's order. Moreover, in this socioracial scheme, blacks and dark-skinned mulattos had no input into the decision-making process, particularly under an authoritarian regime such as Trujillo's. Challenges to the regime from lower-class sectors were ruthlessly crushed (often after periods of fictitious tolerance); this was the fate of the labor movement in the sugarcane industry (Cassá 1992, 2:271–73).

Antihaitianismo ideology also defended a social-racial model in which only the light-skinned Hispanophile elites really fit. The rest of the Dominican people had to struggle to "whiten" themselves (at least culturally) or were alienated and excluded from the national prototype. Therefore, "whiteness" (racially and culturally) came to be identified with "Dominicanness," while "blackness" was rejected as alien, Haitian, and barbaric. Challenges to the hegemonic power of the state from below could thus be isolated and thwarted as "foreign" or "un-Dominican."

In this (re)definition of "race," the black and mulatto masses had but two choices: to "lighten" themselves by assuming the indio identity and Hispanic culture, or to be ostracized and excluded from the national mainstream. The survival of so many Afro-Caribbean elements in contemporary Dominican culture attests to the limited effectiveness of the Trujillista ideological onslaught among the people, and to their heroic resistance (Torres-Saillant 1998). Still, cultural defiance had its price during the Trujillo era, and most Dominicans simply acquiesced (at least publicly) to the power of the state. Finally, antihaitianismo ideology and its definition of race provided a compensatory mechanism from oppression for the dark-skinned lower classes. When compared to Haitians, dark-skinned Dominicans could feel racially and culturally superior. As antihaitianismo ideology sought to blur their racial consciousness (blacks and mulattos were replaced by indios), it offset the loss by giving them a national consciousness. Race was now a "national" matter: Haitians—and only Haitians—were black, and Dominicans were not.

The Dominican racial pyramid during the Trujillo era looked extremely complex and contradictory. There were many "whites" at the top, though most Dominicans were racially mixed.[7] The bulk of the pyramid comprised a rainbow of mulatto hues, most of them classified as indio, and finally there were practically no blacks at the bottom, or at least very few Dominican blacks, for *black* had become a term associated solely with Haiti (Charles 1992, 150–51).

Racial mobilization improved little during the Trujillo era. Some mulattos and blacks made it to positions of power, usually through the army or governmental positions. For example, Trujillo, his relatives, and his de segunda cronies were mostly light-skinned mulattos. And in spite of Trujillo's overwhelming control over the Dominican economy, he never truly broke the power of the oligarchy; he simply forced the elites to give him the lion's share of the economy and to (often unwillingly) take him on as a business partner. He also forced them to open their exclusive social clubs (from which Trujillo had been rejected in the past) to Trujillo's close collaborators. Trujillo and his courtiers thus associated in business, social gatherings, and even marriage with these traditional elites. As a result, Dominican racial stratification remained relatively unchanged, with only a small Trujillista elite moving to the top.

The Legacy of Trujillo

For almost thirty-one years the Dominican people were subjected to the ideological bombardment of the Trujillo regime. Using the work of the country's best intellectuals, the support of the Catholic Church, and the state machinery, Trujillo reproduced antihaitianismo ideology throughout the national territory. So pervasive and effective was this propaganda barrage that it was difficult for any Dominican not to be influenced by it.

The effectiveness of the regime's antihaitianismo ideology lay in the fact that it was easily accepted by Dominicans; it had been part of Dominican culture since colonial times. For decades before the advent of Trujillo, many Dominicans had falsely believed that they were white, Hispanic, and Catholic, while only Haitians were black (Moya Pons 1986b, 245). What the Trujillo regime did was to take antihaitianismo ideology to new intellectual and political heights by making it a state-sponsored ideology. Antihaitianismo ideology received the full backing of the powerful Trujillista state and was infused with new life and coherence by intellectuals such as Peña Batlle and Balaguer. Not even the everyday existence of common Dominicans was spared from the influence of antihaitianismo ideology, as it reached into popular customs and entertainment. Without any doubt, the Trujillo era marks the zenith of antihaitianismo in the Dominican Republic. No administration before or after Trujillo gave antihaitianismo ideology such strong support. Not surprisingly, just as vestiges of *Trujillismo* still show up in Dominican culture and politics, so does antihaitianismo maintain a clear presence in Dominican society. The myth was institutionalized.

4

Antihaitianismo Ideology in the Post-Trujillo Period

Though antihaitianismo is no longer the state's official ideology, as it was during the Trujillo era, the tenets of antihaitianismo are still widely employed throughout Dominican society and in its political discourse. For thirty-one years, the Trujillo regime fashioned vacuous political institutions while trying to shape the minds of the Dominican people. Its legacy of authoritarianism, personalism, and lack of political institutionalization continues to affect Dominican society, and antihaitianismo ideology is a notorious part of it. Anti-Haitian prejudice and discrimination are commonplace in contemporary Dominican society, and antihaitianismo ideology has become a favorite weapon in the hands of pseudonationalist politicians.

This chapter examines the contemporary manifestations and reproduction of antihaitianismo ideology in the Dominican Republic. It covers, first, the "new" antihaitianismo literature and its theoretical constructions; second, the widespread reproduction of antihaitianismo ideology in Dominican society through socialization, education, the media; and, finally, the prevalence of anti-Haitian attitudes among the general public and Dominican elites (as expressed in surveys and field interviews).

The "New" Antihaitianismo Literature

After the Trujillo regime ended, antihaitianismo ideology took new forms. Deep psychological scars had been produced by the dictatorship, and these were manipulated by some of the dictator's former ideologues and collaborators, most notably Joaquín Balaguer. Contemporary or post-Trujillo antihaitianismo has stronger nationalist and cultural overtones, while downplaying the racial issue. The civil rights struggles of the 1960s discredited overtly racist thought, forcing anti-Haitian ideologues to resort to subtler approaches. Writers like Joaquín Balaguer, Carlos Cornielle, Luis Julián Pérez, and Manuel Núñez (among others) promote a particular brand of Dominican ultranationalism laden with heavy doses of antihaitianismo ideology. Furthermore, they portray the Dominican Republic as the affected party in the Haitian-Dominican relationship and Haiti as the offending party. Although some of these writers belong to the Trujillista "old guard," others, like Manuel Núñez, are part of a new generation of anti-Haitian nationalists.

Luis Julián Pérez, for example, served in Trujillo's administration from 1945 to 1961. In his book *Santo Domingo frente al destino* (Santo Domingo Facing Destiny), published in 1990, he presents Haitians as aggressors and as the main cause of the Dominican Republic's historical conflicts. He even blames the 1937 massacre on Haitians' insatiable greed for land and resources (1990, 91). Pérez also absolves Trujillo's bureaucrats from any responsibility for the massacre and instead blames the incident solely on Trujillo. He then proceeds to absolve Trujillo himself to some degree, claiming the dictator was the victim of historical and political circumstances (1990, 99). Finally, Pérez warns the Dominican people that the "Haitian problem" is reaching alarming proportions, and unless something is done to stop it, there could be a new wave of violence (1990, 104).[1] Pérez's writings lack the sophistication of other anti-Haitian ideologues, and his arguments are simple repetitions of old "issues."

Joaquín Balaguer's "new" brand of antihaitianismo is detailed in his controversial best-seller *La isla al revés* (The Upside Down Island).[2] *La isla al revés* (1984) is basically a modified and updated version of *La realidad dominicana* (1947), from which entire sections have been copied. In this "new" work, Balaguer once again defends the Dominican case. The Dominican Republic, he argues, has the historical misfortune of living next to Haiti. Still, the Dominican Republic has been miraculously able to maintain its Hispanic-Catholic culture in the face of Haitian penetration (1984, 63).

As in *La realidad dominicana,* in *La isla al revés* Balaguer presents a distorted view of Dominican history to further his cause: "The extinction of the Indian race should have given rise to the population of Santo Domingo to be integrally constituted by European families, specially Spanish and French. Before the Treaty of Basel (1795), the colony's population was formed by the best of the families that had migrated to America, attracted by gold or by the fascinating mystery of remote expeditions" (1984, 59). In this brief passage, Balaguer helps perpetuate the myth of the white Dominican by ignoring the fact that well before 1795 the colony of Santo Domingo was mostly made up of blacks and mulattos (Cassá 1992, 1:89; Moya Pons 1977, 378–79). Balaguer's romantic notion of Dominican history is, unfortunately, still shared by many Dominicans.

Also widely shared are his nineteenth-century notions of racial differences: "The Negro, abandoned to his instincts, and without the restraint on reproduction that a relatively high level of living imposes on all countries, multiplies himself with a speed similar to that of vegetable species" (1984, 36). Balaguer's bigotry is not limited to Haitians but includes all members of the black race. Moreover, Balaguer conveniently obviates the fact that blacks constitute a significant part of the Dominican population. Or is he trying to imply that Dominicans are not black? It seems that Balaguer is simply appealing to the myth of the nonblack, Dominican Indian. For example, the book includes a section of color pictures in which Balaguer portrays the "real," "untouched" Dominicans: white peasants from the central highlands.

Balaguer then deals further with these issues and becomes more specific and crude:

The de-nationalization of Santo Domingo, persistently realized for over a century through trading with the worst of the Haitian population, has made alarming progress. Our racial origin and our Hispanic nation's tradition must not divert us from recognizing that our nationality is in danger of disintegrating if drastic measures are not employed against the menace that represents the neighboring Haitian nation. The first sign of this de-nationalization is constituted by the increasing ethnic decadence of the Dominican population. Contact with the [Haitian] Negro has contributed, without any doubt, to the slackening of our public manners. (1984, 45)

The influence of Haiti has also had a disintegrative effect on the Dominican soul. The continuous flow of foreigners of the black race, constantly mixing with the lower classes of society . . . has broken down patriotic feelings and the feeling of national solidarity. (1984, 48)

Equally important to Balaguer's ideas are two related facts. First, he has been president of the Dominican Republic on seven occasions. The author of *La isla al revés* is not an obscure writer but an individual who has the power, prestige, and influence to reproduce these views among the Dominican people. Second, *La isla al revés* became an instant national bestseller, which suggests that the topic of the book appealed to the public and that many educated Dominicans share Balaguer's views.

In his 1990 book *El ocaso de la nación dominicana* (The Twilight of the Dominican Nation), Manuel Núñez tries to rescue some of the old Trujillista ideas about nationalism and antihaitianismo by employing the cultural argument. In order for the Dominican Republic to survive as a distinct cultural entity in the face of Haitian aggression, he argues, decisive steps must be taken (1990, 310–11). This time it is not the racial purity of the Dominican nation that is at stake (as Balaguer would argue), but rather its cultural homogeneity. Haitian migration is inexorably diluting Dominican culture, according to Núñez:

We have lived turning our backs to an essential, crucial problem, for the future, not of nationality, but for the future of that which has constituted up to now an authentic safeguard and strength: for dominicanidad [Dominicanness]. The Haitian [migrant] does not adapt to our culture, but penetrates and transforms it, revolutionizes its customs, its language, its values, its habits, its beliefs. From the contact between both cultures, the Haitian [culture] comes out unscathed. We are facing a process of mutation that has all the characteristics of an irreversible fact. Not because the prevalent tendencies cannot be reversed, but because the causes that provoke the Haitian exodus toward the Dominican Republic do not seem to cease. (1990, 310–11)

To make his case stronger, Núñez also launches personal vendettas against revisionist historians (such as Roberto Cassá, Rubén Silié, Franklin J. Franco, and Emilio Cordero Michel), accusing them of being poor scholars, unDominican, pro-Haitian, and even Marxist imperialists (1990, 130–32). Núñez argues that these revisionist historians are nothing but distorters of

Dominican history, who embellish the Haitian occupation, ignoring or overlooking the real facts.

These examples show that Haitian culture is perceived by neoantihaitianismo ideology, first, as alien, and second, as pernicious and contaminating. Dominican culture is still portrayed as Spanish, Christian, and Catholic; not African and voodoo-worshiping. Moreover, the new anti-Haitian ideologues present culture as homogenous, static, and immutable. When they talk about "Dominican culture," they refer to an idealized Hispanic-based conception of Dominicanness that developed centuries ago and remains in place, except for the threat that it faces from Haiti. In other words, Dominican culture has its roots firmly planted in the white and progressive Western civilization, and more specifically, in the Hispanic world, whereas Haitian culture represents the black and backward civilizations of a primitive (not to say barbaric) Africa.

Thus Dominican culture, as seen by neoantihaitianismo ideology, is clearly "superior," and any contact with or influence from the Haitian culture can only have detrimental effects for the Dominican Republic. The agent of this cultural penetration is, of course, the Haitian migrant, who enters the Dominican Republic and stays in the country. In short, antihaitianismo ideology is far from dead. New generations of Dominican intellectuals keep it alive by reproducing the same old myths and prejudiced arguments in slightly altered "new" forms.

Socialization and Antihaitianismo

Antihaitianismo ideology is part of a set of attitudes that are acquired early in life and reinforced by the socialization process. Family and friends are the first agents of this socialization process. Just as they were taught, they teach children the basic tenets of antihaitianismo ideology. Their actions are a mere reflection of a process that is repeated from generation to generation. Attitudes acquired during childhood tend to have lasting effects. The early childhood years are "critical for developing personality, social attitudes, and cultural values," and "racial awareness appears to develop in the preschool years" (Dawson and Prewitt 1969, 41, 47).

Equally important is the role played by public education in this process. Public education, unlike the teachings of family and friends, is not a loose, uncoordinated, and incomplete process. Public education is a coordinated and formative process. It is institutionalized and supported by the state and has as its main objective the formation of tomorrow's Dominican citizens. In school Dominican children learn historical "facts" that they identify with and reproduce later in life.

Unfortunately, what most Dominican children learn at school is a national history full of distortions, myths, and prejudices (F. J. Franco 1979, 149).[3] Elementary school textbooks emphasize the Indian and Spanish heritages, while barely mentioning the role of blacks in Dominican society. One textbook asserts that the language of the Dominican people is a mix of Spanish and Taíno; another states that the Dominican people inherited a new race from the Spanish (González Canalda and Silié 1985, 22, 23).

An examination of Dominican history books from the late nineteenth century to the present reveals a number of flagrant errors, romantic myths, and anti-Haitian biases. Several generations of Dominican intellectuals were influenced by these books, which set the tone for the teaching of history at educational institutions. One of the most common myths present in traditional Dominican history texts is that of messianism. For example, Juan Pablo Duarte, the nation's leading hero and intellectual author of Dominican independence, is glorified to extremes. Joaquín Balaguer even compares him to Jesus Christ:

> The father of the Fatherland had a conscience enticed by the figure of Christ and made in the image of that sublime redeemer of the human family. (1994, 224)

> Duarte would sometimes speak like Jesus and many of his sentences seem spoken from a mountain of the Bible. (1994, 226)

Another common historical myth is that of the intervention of the Divine Providence on the side of Dominicans. After exalting the brilliant victories of the Dominican troops in the face of the more numerous Haitian army, Balaguer adds: "The fact of [our] survival is one of those miracles that prove the wisdom and kindness with which Providence governs the events of the historic world" (1984, 63).

Dominican history textbooks also portray Haitians as the eternal enemies of the Dominican people. The Haitian invasions of Toussaint and Dessalines, the Haitian occupation (1822–44), and the Haitian-Dominican wars are the subjects of much discussion, which usually emphasizes gory examples of Haitian atrocities. Moreover, these significantly different events are all equated and presented as part of Haiti's historical designs to take over the Dominican Republic. Haitians are portrayed as barbaric savages who were the living incarnation of cruelty and whose only objective was to destroy all traces of Hispanic culture among the Dominican people. For example, Jean-Jacques Dessalines is described as a "heroic monster that surpassed with his boldness and cruelty the boundaries that separate man from beast" (Balaguer 1962, 12). Dessalines's invasion in 1805 is graphically described by various Dominican historians in the following way:

The destruction, the burning, and the killing were the wake that Haitians left in their retreat. (Gimbernard 1974, 178)

The priest Don Juan Vásquez suffered a cruel death: he was burned alive in the chorus' balcony, using as tinder the benches and other combustible objects of the church. (Monte y Tejada [1853] 1953, 244)

The road that goes from Santiago to Cap Haïtien was covered with dead bodies, and like errant shadows, children who looked in vain for their parents were seen. (Pichardo 1966, 67)

Scenes of horror frequently alternated with those of death, infused anxiety and fear into those who survived to face new disgraces, and to give testimony of the consummation of horrendous crimes. (Logroño 1912, 162)

. . . Quenching their brutal furor on that harmless attendance, from which very few were left alive, because even the officiating priest was spiked by their bayonets, in the middle of the horrendous uproar of that horde of savages. (García [1878] 1968, 1:319)

In other cases, such as the *Historia gráfica de la República Dominicana* (Illustrated History of the Dominican Republic; [1944] 1986), by José Ramón Estella and José Alloza,[4] the text is accompanied by detailed drawings in which Haitians are portrayed with crude and apelike features, while Dominicans are always drawn light-skinned and with European features. As a result of this manipulation and distortion of Dominican history in school, Dominican children acquire these attitudes and beliefs early in life and make them their own. They will grow up, first, despising and discriminating against Haitians for their past atrocities, second, perceiving themselves as light-skinned Hispanics vis-à-vis the Haitian black, and third, rejecting blackness as alien and barbaric. Early in life, a cultural wedge is driven into the minds of Dominican children by which they learn to distinguish between "us" and the alien "others" (that is, Haitians).

This "false consciousness" is perpetuated by the Dominican government, which has institutionalized many of the racist elements of Dominican culture. For example, the Dominican government uses the term *indio* as a skin color descriptor in the national identity card that every adult Dominican must carry (see appendix A for examples).[5] As a result, *indio* is no longer a slang term; it has become an official racial category, accepted and used by the Dominican government for identification and classification purposes. Most Dominicans fall within the indio category, with gradations for lighter or darker skin tones (*indio claro* or *indio oscuro*). White or light-skinned Dominicans are labeled *blanco* (white), while dark-skinned Dominicans are usually labeled *moreno.* Inclusion in one category or another may also be influenced by the individual's facial features (nose, lips, and hair texture, for example). But very few Dominicans are actually labeled *negro* (black), due to the term's pejorative connotations in Dominican society.

Antihaitianismo in the Media

The print and broadcast media also contribute to the reproduction of antihaitianismo ideology in Dominican society. With an adult literacy rate of 83 percent, the Dominican Republic has nine daily newspapers, more than any other Caribbean or Central American nation (Goodwin 1998, 120). But access to the media in the Dominican Republic is limited; only the well-known, well-connected, and/or well-educated can communicate their ideas through the media. Other social groups have no access to the media, or their message is filtered, censored, and/or edited by those in control of the media. According to van Dijk, "None of the other power elites, and specially the political elites, and their discourses could be as influential as they are without the mediating and sometimes reinforcing functions of the press, radio, and television" (1993, 241). While the media play an important role in developing feelings of national identity in many developing countries, in the Dominican Republic they also help to reproduce biased or prejudiced elite dogmas, particularly the dominant ideology of antihaitianismo.

Not surprisingly, Haiti and Haitian migrants are portrayed in the Dominican media in an unfavorable way. Haiti-related news stories in the Dominican media consist of three types: news about the domestic political situation in Haiti itself, news about Haitian-Dominican relations, and news about Haitians in the Dominican Republic. Given the presumed importance that the Dominican media assign to Haiti, it is surprising that not a single Dominican newspaper has a permanent correspondent in Port-au-Prince. News from Haiti reaches the Dominican media by way of international press agencies (Caroit 1992, 29), such as Associated Press (AP) or, more recently, Centro Puente. These agencies, of course, just cover events that are relevant for their immediate public back home. As a result, the only kind of "news" about Haiti that is actually produced in the Dominican Republic consists of the editorials and commentaries that appear in Dominican newspapers on a periodical basis, a practice which is not conducive to objective reporting. Most Dominican reporters have little knowledge about Haiti, and they tend to write their news stories from foreign or secondary sources. So far, there are only three experienced Dominican reporters with some firsthand knowledge about Haiti: Leo Reyes from *El Nacional,* and Germán Reyes and Pastor Vásquez from *Hoy.*

News stories about Haiti are usually also highlighted with alarmist headlines, so as to have a powerful impact on the reader and stimulate sales (see, for example, CIPROS 1992, 145–48). This practice is common, particularly among the afternoon papers, like *Última Hora,* because Haiti-related news sells newspapers (Dominican journalist, personal communication). Therefore, news about Haiti is given priority, and news about political violence in Haiti or controversies about Haitian migrants in the Dominican Republic usually makes it to the front page.

Most of the editorials, commentaries, and letters to the editor dealing with "the Haitian problem" that I examined contained an anti-Haitian bias. Though editorials are generally phrased in a moderate and tactful language, during times of tensions, such as when Haitian president Jean-Bertrand Aristide denounced the Dominican Republic at the United Nations in 1991, editorials have followed the tenets of the dominant discourse of antihaitianismo ideology. Commentaries and letters to the editor are even more anti-Haitian, since in this case the integrity of the newspaper is not at risk.

If a picture is worth a thousand words, then political cartoons are a relevant part of the written media.[6] Political cartoons usually imply feelings that are too strong or controversial to be printed, and in the case of the Dominican media, they offer an interesting and perceptive insight into antihaitianismo. A selection of political cartoons from Dominican newspapers reflects a strong anti-Haitian bias (see appendix B for some examples). These political and editorial cartoons speak for themselves and represent a poignant example of the reproduction of antihaitianismo ideology in the Dominican mass media. Moreover, some of these cartoons are blatantly racist, with black characters seemingly taken from the United States' "Old South." Haitians are traditionally stereotyped as destitute blacks, whereas Dominicans and the Dominican Republic are portrayed in favorable terms, usually by white figures. The message that these cartoons convey is simple and unequivocal: Haitians are black, Dominicans are not; Haiti is a trouble spot, therefore, the Dominican Republic must always be on the alert regarding Haiti's potential threat.

Since Haitians in the Dominican Republic have little access to the media, there is not much that they can do to defend themselves. Some Haitians do not speak or understand Spanish well. Others, such as borderland Haitians and Haitian Dominicans, even though they have mastered Dominican Spanish, are often considered Haitians and thus denied any access to the media. Most Haitians in the Dominican Republic are also poor and illiterate, plus they fear voicing their opinions, since they are foreigners who may be subjected to deportation (particularly if they are illegal aliens). Only some individuals, human rights organizations, and religious groups have tried to give Haitians a voice. For their part, most of the Dominican media have chosen to ignore or understate the plight of Haitians.

Anti-Haitian Attitudes among the General Public

This section is based on fifteen focus group interviews (with eight to ten participants in each group) that I conducted with individuals in the cities of Santo Domingo and Santiago, in the sugar industry in the southwest, and in the borderland; it also draws on surveys and studies carried out by other researchers.

During my field research I found that attitudes—at least those vocalized by lower-class and lower-middle class Dominicans—toward Haiti and Haitians in the Dominican Republic are mostly negative. Most Dominicans, even those who live and work closely with Haitians, expressed public feelings of dislike and distrust toward Haitians. These observations correspond with data collected by other researchers (Equipo Onè-Respe [a religious group that seeks to promote a better understanding of Haitian-Dominican relations] 1995; S. Martínez 1997; Vega 1993b; Wilhelms 1994). Respondents sought to justify their antihaitianismo in different ways, but all their explanations have one element in common: Haiti and Haitians living in the Dominican Republic represent a threat in one way or another.

Of the three theoretical models discussed in the introduction—the sociocultural model, the symbolic racism model, and the racial threats model—I found that anti-Haitian attitudes among the general public in the Dominican Republic are best represented by the sociocultural model, followed by the symbolic racism model. History and culture—or more specifically, the way in which they have been manipulated—have clearly played an important part in the development and reproduction of antihaitianismo ideology in the Dominican Republic, which is a truly social phenomenon. Therefore, I divided the data collected during my interviews according to van Dijk's (1987) model, which treats prejudice as a socially shared and reproduced phenomenon.

As discussed in the introduction, prejudice can be classified on the basis of three dimensions of threat: economic, cultural, and social (van Dijk 1987, 58–60). These three dimensions of threat, especially the last two, surfaced during my interviews. Furthermore, anti-Haitian attitudes expressed by lower-class Dominicans generally conformed to van Dijk's five prejudice categories: immigration, crime and aggression, unfair competition, cultural conflicts, and personal characteristics (1987, 364–66). Under the immigration category, van Dijk points to the constant references made by speakers about a "flood" of immigrants. Under the crime and aggression category, he includes references to the migrants as the agents responsible for increasing crime rates. In the unfair competition category, the main prejudice is the widespread belief that migrant workers "steal" jobs from native residents. In the cultural conflicts category, most prejudices depict foreign cultures as "strange," "different," or "inferior." Finally, in the personal characteristics category, immigrants are portrayed as stupid, lazy, uneducated, backward, childish, and so forth (van Dijk 1987, 364–66). Following van Dijk's approach, I divided the results of my focus group interviews into the same five categories.

In comparison with van Dijk's study of the Netherlands, Dominicans have more intense and overtly racist attitudes. Even though van Dijk also interviewed lower-class Dutch, their opinions seem "soft" and even moderate when compared to those of lower-class Dominicans. This is even more remarkable when we consider the fact that Dominicans have more in common with Haitians, due to geographic proximity, history, and miscegenation, than the Dutch do with Turkish, Moroccan, or Surinamese migrants. There are plausible explanations for this. First, van Dijk's lower-class Dutch respondents were probably better educated than most of my Dominican respondents and thus would be less inclined to publicly express overtly racist opinions. And second, it is precisely these commonalities between Haitians and Dominicans that antihaitianismo ideology aims to eradicate. For most anti-Haitian ideologues, Haiti and the Dominican Republic (increasingly) have too much in common, more than they would like to acknowledge. Antihaitianismo ideology thus strives to drive a cultural wedge between Haitians and Dominicans by emphasizing their differences, rather than their commonalities.

Immigration prejudices are, as expected, some of the most obvious. Certain groups, such as Dominicans in the sugar industry, live in a social setting where they are outnumbered by Haitians. During the sugar harvest season, the great majority of field workers (about 65 percent) are Haitians or of Haitian ancestry, while Dominicans perform semispecialized tasks (as drivers, guards, mechanics) or administrative jobs (Murphy 1991, 70). Still, all groups perceived Haitian migration as an out-of-control situation, a kind of invasion threatening them and their country, and they expressed these prejudices very clearly:

We are being invaded!

Half the country's [the Dominican Republic's] population is already Haitian. They [Haitians] are preparing [to take over]. They are close to a million and they are surrounding the whole country.

We are afraid that they [Haitians] may invade us [Dominicans].

This place [the Dominican Republic] is theirs; they are going to take over this country.

They [Haitians] say that [the territory] from Azua to the border belongs to Haiti. Every day more of them arrive; it is a massive invasion.

They [Haitians] live here as in paradise; they have become the owners of this country.

These typical examples of the immigration prejudice are alarmist in nature and not supported by the facts. They seem more like general allegations based on hearsay or simplistic reproductions of antihaitianismo ideology. For instance, when asked about the number of Haitians living in the Dominican Republic, most respondents answered "a lot," "too many," or the vague figure of "more than a million."[7]

According to lower-class Dominicans, not only are a large number of Haitians living in the Dominican Republic, but they are staking a claim on Dominican territory by maintaining they own the border region up to Azua. This prejudice originates in the long-standing dispute over the borderland between Haiti and the Dominican Republic. While some Dominicans still claim Haiti's central plateau as a former part of the Dominican Republic, some Haitian leaders have claimed the southern borderland as part of Haiti (Fignolé 1948). Therefore, this prejudice clearly is rooted in official discourse and is reproduced, in a very vague and imprecise manner, by lower-class Dominicans.

Finally, Haitian migrants are perceived as being part of a conspiracy to take over the Dominican Republic. According to this notion, since Haiti lacks the military means to enforce its territorial claims on the Dominican Republic, it has resorted to a different strategy: a demographic invasion. Simply put, Haitians will continue to spill over the border until they outnumber Dominicans, and then they will realize their long-standing dream of unifying the island. Again, this perception is part of the dominant discourse of antihaitianismo ideology and has little to do with the everyday experience of the respondents. Most of the respondents failed to perceive Haitian migration as a natural phenomenon of Caribbean societies or as a purely economic phenomenon (S. Martínez 1995). Rather, they interpreted Haitian migration through the distorted lens of antihaitianismo ideology. Haitian migration is perceived to be part of a hidden, political agenda. It must be planned or organized in some way from Haiti, as it cannot be a collection of individual decisions.

Crime and aggression prejudices were the least reported in my interviews. Crime rates are low in the Dominican Republic, and the National Police is generally feared for its harshness. Only among sugar industry workers did this prejudice surface in a consistent manner. This finding is easily understood when one considers that working and living conditions in the sugar industry are among the worst in the country, and both Haitians and Dominicans must work hard to make a living, often coming in conflict with each other. Though the prejudice of these Dominicans (in particular in the sugar industry) was often based on personal experiences (quarrels with Haitians, work-related conflicts), their justifications were not:

They [Haitians] are the kind of people that if a Dominican happens to offend one of them, then they will all beat up the Dominican to defend their fellow men, their nation.

They [Haitians] want to kill you with a machete or with witchcraft. Evil is in their nationality. That [evil] comes from Haiti.

Haitians mistreat women; they beat them.

Fights and quarrels, within and between national groups, are not an uncommon occurrence in the harsh world of the sugar plantation. Dominican workers, however, utilized antihaitianismo ideology to portray Haitians as the sole wrongdoers and the root of all problems. Furthermore, they perceived Haitians as inherently evil. Finally, though most Dominicans denied believing in witchcraft, they did admit that evil exists and that Haitians, as the carriers of this evil into the Dominican Republic, were capable of harming them. None of the respondents could provide conclusive evidence to support these allegations. Instead, most of them reported, "I heard that it happened to someone."

The role of antihaitianismo as a dominant ideology was particularly evident in this prejudice category. Respondents publicly voiced their fears of Haitians, even though they did not correspond to reality. In most cases, the respondents interacted daily with Haitians without any serious conflicts. A poignant example was the case of a Dominican worker who, even though he was a vocal Haitian-basher, was married to a Haitian woman. When I asked him to explain this apparent contradiction, he answered, "I sleep with one eye open and the other one closed" (meaning that he did not trust her completely since she was a Haitian). This divergence between public concerns and everyday reality again points to the social nature of antihaitianismo ideology.

In the Dominican Republic, the crime and aggression prejudice differs from van Dijk's findings for the Netherlands. Haitians are not specifically perceived as the cause of a rising crime wave. To the contrary, Haitians living on the state sugar plantations are tightly controlled by the Dominican military and plantation guards. Haitians are perceived as *potential* criminals, not only because they supposedly fight in groups, but also because they know the secrets of voodoo and witchcraft, which they can use to carry out a painful vengeance. These popular notions of Haitian witchcraft and voodoo can also be found in the Dominican media, in newspapers as prestigious as the *Listín Diario* (Vallejo 1993). For most of the respondents, voodoo and witchcraft were the same thing. Few, if any, had any precise notions of what voodoo religion really was (also reported by Equipo Onè-Respe 1995, 99–101). Still, lower-class Dominicans fear the potential harm that Haitians are capable of inflicting on them, even though many of them have not actually witnessed this. In conclusion, given the low correlation between this prejudice and the everyday experience of the respondents, it can be assumed that they are just reproducing a prejudice acquired elsewhere.

The charge of unfair competition was again more pronounced in Dominicans in the sugar industry, where living conditions were the worst. It did surface among respondents in the major cities (particularly construction workers) and in the borderland, but these respondents had more employment options than Dominicans working in the sugar industry. For example, urban Dominicans could work in other economic sectors (free trade zones, street peddling, et cetera), and borderland Dominicans could make money from agriculture and contraband. But those Dominicans in the sugar industry had no choice but to work for "the company," where they had to interact with Haitians on a daily basis and under stressful conditions. Many of those interviewed viewed Haitians as foreigners who had come illegally and were "stealing" jobs from Dominicans:

If someone pays thirty pesos for some work, a Haitian does it for ten.

The CEA [Consejo Estatal del Azúcar] brings in *amba fil* [illegal] Haitians, and that is why we Dominicans are starving; we just cannot compete. There are Haitian overseers who earn more money than

Dominicans. They earn fifty pesos per day, and I only earn twenty something.

Haitians take away jobs from us because they are in need.

They [Haitians], with the money that they make here, . . . buy foodstuffs, carry them away [to Haiti], and then these products become more expensive. The scarcity of tomato sauce and sugar is because they [Haitians] take them to Haiti.

As noted above, unfair competition is one of the few prejudices that stems from the everyday experiences of the respondents. For example, Dominican sugar workers felt that the use of Haitian migrant workers lowered wages, since Haitians would work for wages that most Dominicans would reject. They even argued that they were willing to cut sugarcane, but not at the current wages. So, according to their view, and indirectly at least, Haitians were not only lowering wages but also effectively barring Dominicans from jobs as sugarcane cutters.

The perception of unfair competition, however, is not entirely economic. The problem is twofold: Dominicans are "losing" jobs (economic justification), but they are "losing" them to Haitians (anti-Haitian prejudice). The fact that it is Haitians who are "stealing" those jobs is, for most of these respondents, an additional insult. The use of Haitian labor has been publicly blamed by Dominican leaders for lowering wages and depopulating the Dominican countryside, among other evils.

The reality is different and not as simple. Studies have shown: first, that Dominicans refuse to cut sugarcane, not only for economic but also for cultural reasons (for example, extremely hard work, slavelike working conditions); and second, that Haitians, in most cases, have entered segments of the job market that Dominicans are abandoning (or are being forced to abandon) in search of better opportunities elsewhere (Grasmuck 1983; Moya Pons 1986a). Since the late nineteenth century, the low wages paid by the sugar plantations made cutting sugarcane unattractive for Dominicans, who could find land or better-paying jobs elsewhere (Vargas-Lundius 1991, 216). The sugar companies were also interested in obtaining a cheaper, more docile immigrant labor force. A similar situation is taking place in other rural economic sectors, such as coffee and rice production, where Haitians are increasing their numbers among the labor force (Lozano and Báez Evertsz 1992; ONAPLAN 1981). Thus antihaitianismo ideology also plays an important role in the unfair competition prejudice by magnifying and distorting an existing labor condition. According to the ultranationalist, anti-Haitian view, it is unfair for a Haitian to earn more money than a Dominican (regardless of his or her experience, skills, or job performance). Haitians are destined to perform hard, manual labor, and to earn less than Dominicans.

Finally, there is the widespread notion that Haitians, with their demand for foodstuffs to take back to Haiti, are causing shortages in the Dominican Republic. But in fact Dominican merchants have until recently had a powerful economic incentive to sell merchandise to Haiti, as they could get much-needed hard currency—either dollars or Haitian gourdes (which were pegged to the dollar at a rate of five gourdes per dollar). In addition, the Dominican military and government officials, who are responsible for controlling trade with Haiti, do not always do their job, since they profit from trade and contraband. So, if anything, the small-scale sale of products to Haitians benefits only the Dominican economy. In this case, antihaitianismo ideology shows more of its contradictions by blindly condemning a practice that generates benefits for the Dominican economy and for local merchant groups.

Cultural prejudices are some of the more widespread manifestations of antihaitianismo ideology. Even those lower-class Dominicans who have little daily interaction with Haitians displayed a strong degree of cultural prejudices. Respondents' notions of Haitian culture are plagued by racial stereotypes, cultural misperceptions, and even blatant bigotry:

Every illegal Haitian should be sent back to his country. [Because] that nation has no friends. It is an evil nation. They [Haitians] are animals.

They [Haitians] are an ungrateful nation by instinct; they would like to be the owners of these bateyes [places where sugarcane workers live].

Every twenty-seventh of February,[8] the [Dominican] government should kill at least five hundred Haitians!

Racism does exist [in the Dominican Republic], but only against the Haitian black. Dominicans hate that nationality, that race. Not because they are black, but because of history. That dates from the time of Trujillo's eviction [of Haitians].[9]

They [Haitians] have bad intentions, due to their race, their nationality.

Even if they [that is, *arrayanos*][10] were born here [in the Dominican Republic], if their parents are Haitian, they are Haitians. That is so by their race and their black blood.

Haitians hate Dominicans. They cannot share anything with anyone. It is an evil nation; they even hate each other. It is the most pernicious nation that there is.

That [tension with Haiti] comes from history. Those [history] books cannot be destroyed by anyone. Haitians used to throw babies up in the air and spike them with their bayonets.[11]

They [Haitians] are dumb and stupid because they are Negroes.

Haitians belong to one race and Dominicans to another.

A Haitian cannot be a soldier in the Dominican Republic, because they [*sic*] bear malice [against Dominicans] that is in their blood.

The tenets of these particular aspects of antihaitianismo ideology are widely shared and taken as undisputed truths (at least publicly) by many lower-class Dominicans. The survey conducted by Equipo Onè-Respe (1995) in Santiago also confirms these observations. Haiti is visualized by many respondents as an intrinsically evil nation, from which nothing good can come. Haitians, by their nationality, are the carriers of this evil into the Dominican Republic.

Second, the concepts of race, nation, and culture lose their meaning until they become one. Haitians are considered black, backward, dumb, and evil, while Dominicans are the opposite. These characteristics then become the trademark of the black race, which is solely identified with Haiti. Evil equals black, which equals Haiti. Black race and black (evil) nation become the same. Moreover, Haitian evil is instinctive, animal-like; "it is in their blood." Dominicans are different. Dominicans, even black

Dominicans, belong to another "race." These beliefs are clearly a popular reproduction of pro-Hispanic antihaitianismo ideology, which portrays the Dominican Republic as a white Hispanic nation and Haiti as a black African nation. Thus, in the particular case of the Dominican Republic, even Dominican blacks can be "whitened" by Hispanic culture until they become clearly differentiated from the "real" blacks: the Haitians. When nation becomes equated with race, as antihaitianismo ideology effectively does, no Dominican has any incentive to consider himself (or herself) black, while all Haitians are labeled as black. Haitians are thus dehumanized, reduced to a deprecated race, the black race (Equipo Onè-Respe 1995, 20–21).

Third, history is manipulated and even distorted by antihaitianismo ideology to support its allegations. Haitian atrocities are emphasized, so as to portray Haitians as evil, as former invaders who could at any time in the future repeat their barbaric acts. Clearly, these perceptions and stereotypes are not supported by the respondents' immediate reality, but rather are the result of anti-Haitian notions learned from other sources and imperfectly reproduced at the local level. Moreover, due to most of the respondents' limited educational background, they have no way of refuting these historical distortions and thus accept them at face value. Similar historical distortions and lack of historical knowledge were found by Equipo Onè-Respe (1995, chap. 3) and S. Martínez (1997).

Finally, antihaitianismo ideology provides lower-class Dominicans with a convenient way of dealing with their conflictive immediate reality. It lets them blame everything bad on Haitians and makes even the poorest of Dominicans feel vastly superior when compared to a poor, black Haitian migrant.

Obviously, antihaitianismo ideology is an excellent "divide and conquer" tactic that diffuses protest. In the minds of Dominican workers, Haitians were to blame for their personal misfortune, not the Balaguer administration. When a few respondents pointed an accusatory finger at the government, it usually was to blame government officials for allowing too many Haitians to enter the country. In essence, the status quo was not objectionable; the corrupt, semiauthoritarian system that subjugates Dominicans was never questioned. Respondents considered their poverty to be a natural, inevitable state that unfair competition from Haitians only worsened. Not surprisingly, it is unlikely that Dominicans and Haitians will make any kind of concerted effort to improve their common lot.

Prejudices regarding personal characteristics are closely related to cultural prejudices, but in this case the target was more the Haitian individual than the Haitian nation. These prejudices target Haitians' appearance, dress, language, and anything else that makes them "different" from Dominicans:

> I would rather throw away the food in my house than give it to one of them [Haitians]. They will not appreciate it.

> They [Haitians] think that we [Dominicans] live here like them [in Haiti].

> They [Haitians] have particular characteristics, like the color of their skin, and their hair. They come from Africa. Dominicans have a well-formed head. They [Haitians], the majority of them, are darker than us [Dominicans]. Their race is African and ours is Spanish. The Spanish race is refined. There is a Haitian genetics; they tend to be darker. I recognize them [Haitians] by their head and their yellow eyes, the color of embers.

> There are cultural differences: the way they [Haitians] dress, dance, walk, and their food.

> In order for me to marry a Haitian he must have a good [economic] position. The black race is less refined. I would not marry a person darker than I am. Good [straight] hair is better than bad [curly] hair. I prefer a poor Dominican over a poor Haitian [for marriage].

> Haitians stink; no amount of perfume will do.

These prejudices, like cultural conflict prejudices, bear little relation to everyday experiences and seek to support Dominican "racial" and cultural superiority. According to some respondents, Haitians could be readily identified by their skin color, their curly hair, and even by the shape of their head. Moreover, they dress differently and emit a foul body odor. The clear objective of this dimension of antihaitianismo ideology is to make Haitians easily classifiable. Dark skin and curly hair would surely equate one with a Haitian and, by extension, with ugliness and evil. Equipo Onè-Respe also found similar responses in its survey (1995, 94–98). As a result of these perceptions, lower-class Dominicans would be inclined to "whiten" themselves by marrying lighter-skinned people, as one respondent proposed.[12] Furthermore, antihaitianismo ideology has imposed a distorted somatic norm in the Dominican Republic where white is beautiful and desirable, while black is ugly, barbaric, and Africanlike. Regardless of the fact that the great majority of the Dominican population is mulatto, the black elements of the Dominican racial composition were seen as shameful, undesirable, or just plain ugly.

The ideology of antihaitianismo is well entrenched among the general public in the Dominican Republic. To a greater or lesser degree, the majority of respondents expressed deep anti-Haitian feelings or, in a more veiled form, a marked preference for "whiteness" at the expense of denigrating the black (that is, Haitian) race. Although racism certainly is a major component of antihaitianismo ideology as expressed by the respondents, race is but one issue. History and culture are also important issues. The central point is that lower-class Dominicans publicly reproduce anti-Haitian prejudices in an imperfect but effective way. Even though most of them could not go into details on historical issues, such as the Haitian occupation of 1822–44, they knew the essential "facts" that allowed them to reproduce the popular myths and stereotypes that surround these events. Those response patterns closely fitted van Dijk's (1987) sociocultural model. In the Dominican Republic, antihaitianismo is socially shared and reproduced by the general public, often (and contradictorily) with little reference to their everyday experience.[13]

The symbolic racism model also helps explain the lack of fit between anti-Haitian attitudes among the general public and their everyday experience. As a matter of fact, it is often difficult to distinguish between the sociocultural model and the symbolic racism model, as both relate to prejudiced attitudes that bear little correspondence to the immediate reality of respondents. The combined application of these two models is a reflection of the complexity of antihaitianismo ideology, which comprises history, culture, race, politics, and economics, and deliberately manipulates and confuses these issues.

The racial threats model proved to be of little value in the examination of anti-Haitian attitudes in the Dominican Republic. The reason is simple: this model is based on actual economic competition between racial groups and leads to rational choice–type decisions (Kinder and Sears 1981, 415). That is not the case in the Dominican Republic. Few of the respondents were actually engaged in any sort of direct economic competition with Haitian migrants. Only Dominican workers in the sugar industry saw themselves as sometimes being displaced from their jobs by Haitian migrants. Still, those Dominican workers were not employed as cane-cutters, which is the activity that utilizes most of the Haitian labor. Furthermore, the respondents' arguments about unfair economic competition were full of references to racial stereotypes and prejudices, further reinforcing the sociocultural and symbolic racism models. The "threat" that Haitians migrants represented was more of a perceived and symbolic threat than actual economic competition. Again, this is what antihaitianismo ideology is all about. Antihaitianismo ideology has thrived on the creation of myths and stereotypes designed to clearly differentiate between Haiti and the Dominican Republic, between Haitian migrants and Dominican nationals, and between a presumed black African culture and white Hispanic values.

Attitudes of the Dominican Elites

It is the main argument of this work that elites are mainly responsible for the creation and reproduction of anti-Haitian attitudes in the Dominican Republic, attitudes that are in turn reproduced by the rest of the Dominican people. The Dominican Republic has a neopatrimonial political system (with fairly free elections, respect for civil rights, free press, and so forth), but it is under the influence of authoritarian power structures and practices (such as personalism, corruption, and clientelism) (Hartlyn 1998a). The majority of the population has very little input into the system, except at election time. Therefore, elites generally influence mass attitudes, not the other way around. As a result, the basic prejudices and attitudes of the general public should be present, at least in a more sophisticated way, at the elite level.

I conducted informal interviews with Dominican elites in the cities of Santo Domingo and Santiago and distinguished two opinion groups, which I labeled "conservatives" and "progressives," following Lil Despradel's usage (1974, 106–7). Though it was sometimes difficult to place an individual in one group or the other, I used the following criteria to distinguish between them. The conservatives held, in one form or another, clear anti-Haitian

Table 1. Views of Dominican Elites Regarding Issues in Haitian-Dominican Relations

Issue	Conservatives	Progressives
Haitian Migration	Serious problem for the Dominican Republic.	Natural trend of Caribbean societies.
Trade with Haiti	Mixed opinions: some in favor, some against it.	Beneficial to the Dominican economy.
Haiti's Environmental Degradation	Serious problem that the Dominican Republic should not shoulder.	The Dominican Republic should help Haiti in solving this problem.
Arrayanos	Haitians by culture.	Dominican citizens.
Race/Ethnicity	Haitians are "darkening" the Dominican Republic.	No racial prejudice.
Haitian Culture	Detrimental to the cultural values of Dominicans.	Tolerant attitude.
Future Relations	Grim outlook.	Hopeful outlook.

attitudes. Most sought to justify their antihaitianismo in terms of history, culture, or the Dominican national interest. This group consisted of twenty individuals, which included government bureaucrats, intellectuals, and journalists. The progressives, on the other hand, tended to be more open-minded and held more unbiased views about Haitians than conservatives, based either on a revisionist (sometimes even Marxist) interpretation of Dominican history or on notions of human rights and solidarity. This group consisted of eleven individuals, including intellectuals, journalists, and directors of nongovernmental organizations (NGOs). Both groups had one thing in common: they were composed of opinion makers, that is, individuals who had access to the media and who could make their views known. Table 1 summarizes the views of these two groups (arranged by topic), as determined by their responses.

For conservatives, the issue of Haitian migration to the Dominican Republic is a serious and long-standing problem. Haitians supposedly take away jobs from Dominicans and are not needed in a country with an already high unemployment and underemployment rate. Progressives see migration as part of a natural trend of Caribbean societies. Just as Dominicans emigrate to the United States and Puerto Rico, so do Haitians come to the Dominican Republic in search of improved living conditions.

Trade was a subject of debate in the conservative camp. While nationalists condemned trade with Haiti, entrepreneurial- minded elites saw it as a sound economic strategy, because Haiti needs practically everything that the Dominican Republic produces. There was no dissension on this issue among the progressives, who favored trade with Haiti.

Haiti's environmental degradation was a thorny issue. While both groups acknowledged Haiti's ecological problems, the conservatives wanted no part in them. According to their view, the Dominican Republic had enough problems of its own to worry about without taking on those of its neighbor. Progressives thought that helping Haiti was a humanitarian cause, one that in the long term would benefit the Dominican Republic. After all, the first country to be affected by Haiti's ecological problems would be the Dominican Republic.

The plight of arrayanos was an even more sensitive matter. For most conservatives, the arrayanos are merely Haitians who happened to have been born on Dominican territory. Progressives, on the other hand, see them as full-fledged Dominican citizens whose rights have to be acknowledged and respected.

Race and culture were, without a doubt, the two issues that provoked the strongest responses in the conservative camp. For many conservatives, the Dominican Republic is not just being physically invaded by Haitian migrants; its culture and values are being undermined and contaminated by alien (that is, Haitian) influences. Some of these conservatives even subscribe to old racial prejudices and see Haitians as inferior beings just for being black. The majority, however, raised only cultural and nationalist objections to the Haitian presence in the Dominican Republic. As racism and bigotry have become unfashionable and not politically correct in today's society, many of these elites have resorted to new forms of discrimination and prejudice. Culture, more than any other thing, has been the target of this renovated antihaitianismo ideology. The progressives, on the other hand, showed little or no racial prejudice and were tolerant of Haitian culture.

Finally, when asked about the future outlook of Haitian-Dominican relations, the conservatives tended to be cautious and reserved, if not pessimistic. For them, Haiti posed a threat to the future of the Dominican Republic. Progressives were more optimistic and pointed to a new era in Haitian-Dominican relations with the election of democratic governments in Haiti and the Dominican Republic, where mutual cooperation would help dispel old tensions.

The conservative and progressive groups were by no means monolithic. Particularly in the conservative camp, variations could be quite extensive, as was the case regarding the trade issue. All conservatives, however, expressed some degree of antihaitianismo in their discourse, and that was the deciding factor for including them in one camp or the other.

These findings are supported by Lil Despradel's (1974) study of ten Dominican historians. Besides clearly identifying two ideological camps (conservatives and progressives), Despradel found a clearly defined generational gap. The "old guard," those between the ages of sixty-two and eighty-five, belonged to the conservative group, while the "new generation," whose ages ranged from thirty-four to fifty-seven, belonged to the progressive camp (L. Despradel 1974, 106–7).

My research did not corroborate that age cleavage, probably for two reasons. First, Despradel's study was conducted more than twenty-five years ago. By now, most of the "old guard" has disappeared and has been replaced by new group members. And second, many of Despradel's "new generation" now falls in the age bracket of the "old guard." Equipo Onè-Respe (1995) also found similar results in its elite interviews.

This traditional elite, which for decades has occupied positions of power and carried out policy decisions in the Dominican Republic, has been responsible for creating, nurturing, and reproducing antihaitianismo ideology. Even though the members of the elite do not comprise a very large group, from their positions of power they have for decades influenced education, popular culture, and the Dominican political culture. Particularly during the Trujillo dictatorship and the Balaguer administrations, they imposed their particular brand of nationalism and transformed antihaitianismo into an ideology for popular consumption.

In conclusion, antihaitianismo is an integral part of Dominican political culture. Both the general public and some Dominican elites (the conservatives) exhibit varying degrees of antihaitianismo. Their antihaitianismo does not seem to correspond to their immediate reality but plays an important role in their daily lives (for the general public) and in their political objectives (for the conservative elites). For the general public, antihaitianismo ideology provides the perfect justification for an unfair state of things, feeds their nationalism, and helps soften their everyday struggle by making them feel superior to Haitian migrants, who are at the bottom of the social pyramid in the Dominican Republic. For the conservative elites, antihaitianismo is an ideological tool for the achievement of political goals and the maintenance of the status quo.

Balaguer and the Cohabitation
of Antihaitianismo with Democracy

Early forms of antihaitianismo ideology linger in the Dominican Republic, even when they are reshaped by contemporary political forces. How the past and the present meet is explained in this chapter. The first half is a historical narrative that examines Haitian-Dominican relations in the post-Trujillo period. Throughout more than three decades and several Dominican administrations, antihaitianismo ideology and domestic politics have been influential factors in the dichotomous Dominican foreign policy toward Haiti. While post-Trujillo Dominican administrations (such as Balaguer's) have often maintained good diplomatic relations with Haiti's authoritarian regimes, they have also employed a nationalist, anti-Haitian discourse for public consumption. "Strained" relations and "crises" with Haiti are best for generating a reasonable amount of fear that checks any "militancy" on the part of the lower classes and the political opposition.

The second half of the chapter is an analysis of the role played by antihaitianismo in Dominican electoral politics. Particularly during the 1994 and 1996 presidential elections, antihaitianismo ideology seemed to enjoy a revival when an anti-Haitian campaign was employed to undermine the popularity of José F. Peña Gómez, the candidate of the Partido Revolucionario Dominicano (PRD). The discussion emphasizes that antihaitianismo ideology still permeates domestic politics in the Dominican Republic, as witnessed during the 1994 and 1996 elections, when anti-Haitian political propaganda was rampant. The chapter concludes with a discussion of the links between foreign and domestic politics in the Dominican Republic. The thesis of the chapter is that antihaitianismo ideology continues to be an important force in the Dominican Republic.

Trujillo and Papa Doc

The dictatorial regime of Rafael Trujillo ushered in a new era in Haitian-Dominican relations, a period characterized by the military preeminence of the Dominican Republic and by Trujillo's active meddling in Haitian politics. While the Dominican Republic has remained militarily more powerful than Haiti, Dominican administrations after Trujillo have not followed his aggressive policies toward Haiti. But even before Trujillo was assassinated in 1961 by a group of disgruntled ex-collaborators, his influence in Haiti sharply declined as a result of two factors: first, the gradual isolation of his regime by the growing community of Latin American democracies and, belatedly, by the United States; second, the election in 1957 of a nationalist president in Haiti, François "Papa Doc" Duvalier, who was initially hostile toward Trujillo.

Conflicts between Duvalier and Trujillo, two power-hungry dictators who allowed no adversaries, soon emerged. Haitian general Antonio Kébreau, who fled to the Dominican embassy after Duvalier suddenly replaced him as army commander, had been a close associate of Trujillo and ended up in exile in the Dominican Republic. But both dictators soon realized that their common interests were better served if they could agree on an acceptable modus vivendi. After all, they were both under pressure from exile groups who could use their neighbor's territory to stage an invasion.

On 22 December 1958, Trujillo and Duvalier met at Malpasse (on the southern part of the Haitian-Dominican border) and signed a mutual-assistance pact (Black 1986, 120; Heinl and Heinl 1978, 599). Besides their security concerns, Trujillo and Duvalier arranged for the official importation of Haitian cane-cutters into the Dominican Republic, thus renewing a six-year accord signed in 1952 (Castor 1987, 130–31). Duvalier reportedly made $7 million a year under this agreement (Heinl and Heinl 1978, 590), while Trujillo obtained the cheap labor force that he needed for his extensive sugar holdings.

Bosch and the 1963 Crisis

Trujillo's assassination in 1961 brought instability to the Dominican Republic as political and military factions tried to fill the vacuum of power. Under U.S. supervision, free and democratic elections were held in 1962, resulting in the victory of Juan Bosch, presidential candidate of the PRD. Bosch, an ardent anti-Trujillista, had been in exile for over two decades and was part of the Latin American social democratic movement that had previously established democratic governments in Venezuela, Costa Rica, and Puerto Rico. Sworn in on 27 February 1963 (Dominican Independence Day), Bosch was deposed by a military coup less than seven months later, on 25 September 1963 (Latorre 1979, chaps. 4, 5).

The Bosch administration represents one of the most tense and conflictive periods in Haitian-Dominican relations. Bosch's relations with Haiti, or more specifically with the Duvalier regime, were tense, if not outright hostile. Bosch considered Duvalier a ruthless dictator in the same vein as Trujillo and hinted at the possibility of overthrowing his regime. According to Bosch:

> Duvalier constitutes a threat to the peace of the whole continent, and he has demonstrated it when he declared that only God could take power away from him. . . .
>
> I am going to take the initiative in demanding that the nations of the Americas break their diplomatic relations with the Haitian tyrant. Upon the next aggression perpetrated by Haiti, we will inform the OAS [Organization of American States] of our reaction, but we will not do it from here, but from a neighboring capital. (Diederich and Burt 1986, 214)

Duvalier, who considered Bosch "an irresponsible madman," had plotted to have Bosch assassinated and offered asylum in Haiti to notorious Trujillistas and members of the Trujillo family (Heinl and Heinl 1978, 629). On 28 April 1963, the Haitian-Dominican crisis reached new heights. Two days before, the Duvalier children (Simone and Jean-Claude) were shot at while arriving at school. In the attack, only the children's bodyguards were killed with precisely aimed shots—a clear warning to Duvalier. Delirious with rage, Duvalier ordered the elimination of former lieutenant

François Benoît, star member of the army rifle team, notwithstanding the fact that at the time of the incident Benoît was in asylum inside the Dominican embassy (Heinl and Heinl 1978, 630). After killing most of Benoît's family, a group of Duvalier's Tonton Macoutes penetrated the Dominican chancery looking for him, a clear violation of international law. When they could not find Benoît, they moved to the grounds of the Dominican residence, which they surrounded.

Bosch reacted by calling on the OAS to invoke the Rio Treaty (an inter-American collective security pact signed in 1947), presenting Duvalier with a twenty-four-hour ultimatum, and mobilizing Dominican troops at the Haitian border (Tomasek 1968, 294–97). In Santo Domingo, a crowd of students stoned the Haitian embassy, while newspaper editorials gave their unconditional support to Bosch. Even the Haitian consul, Jean-Louis Charles, resigned and requested political asylum in Santo Domingo (Diederich and Burt 1986, 206–9). Only the withdrawal of the troops surrounding the Dominican diplomatic mission and the intervention of the OAS prevented the outbreak of further hostilities.

Following the incident, Duvalier strengthened his position, while Bosch began to confront serious internal problems. The Dominican military, which had always distrusted Bosch and branded him a "leftist," resented his handling of the crisis. They felt that Bosch had manipulated—and exacerbated—the crisis for domestic political gains, while the military had to endure the hardships and risks (Diederich and Burt 1986, 220–21).

Thereafter, with or without Bosch's knowledge,[1] Haitian exiles began training in the Dominican Republic, with the help of the Dominican armed forces. The activities of these exile groups had the effect of escalating the Haitian-Dominican crisis. Haiti countered the Dominican allegations with charges, at the United Nations, of a conspiracy between the Dominican government and Haitian exiles to overthrow the Duvalier government. Duvalier also decided to protect his regime with more extreme measures. He closed the border and ordered the creation of a "war zone," a three-mile-deep strip of scorched earth along the border, where anyone caught crossing it without authorization was to be shot on sight (Diederich and Burt 1986, 236; Heinl and Heinl 1978, 638).

In the Dominican Republic, several groups of Haitian exiles under the leadership of former general Léon Cantave prepared themselves for the overthrown of Duvalier. In August and September of 1963, Cantave's irregular forces launched a series of small attacks on Haitian villages, all of them unsuccessful, after which they retreated to Dominican territory. The last attack took place on the morning of 23 September 1963 and was directed toward the Haitian army outpost at Ouanaminthe (known as Juana Méndez in Spanish—across the Masacre River from the Dominican town of Dajabón). Apparently, the Haitian government troops had been alerted in advance. Cantave's men quickly retreated across the river into the Dominican Republic.

In pursuit, the Haitian troops fired into the town of Dajabón, an action interpreted by the Bosch administration as an act of war. Bosch sent an ultimatum to Duvalier, ordering him to cease all hostilities and warning that Dominican troops might attack Port-au-Prince in response. Bosch also ordered an investigation into the incident by a commission of the Dominican armed forces and by the OAS (Diederich and Burt 1986, 256–58). Neither inquiry got past the preliminary stage, as Juan Bosch was overthrown by a military coup on 25 September 1963.

Balaguer and the Duvaliers

Although Haitian-Dominican relations did not fully normalize until 1966, Bosch's ouster defused a potentially explosive situation. Not since 1937 had Haiti and the Dominican Republic been so close to the brink of war. Still, antihaitianismo ideology did not play a role in the conflict. Bosch's opposition to Duvalier stemmed from his well-known antidictatorial beliefs. He saw in Duvalier another Trujillo, one who, in fact harbored Trujillista exiles.

The unstable nature of Dominican politics, from Bosch's overthrow in 1963 to the U.S. military intervention in the country in 1965, was a major factor in delaying the normalization of Haitian-Dominican relations. After the U.S. military intervened, elections were held in 1966. The winner was Joaquín Balaguer of the Partido Reformista (PR). Balaguer, a former high-level public official and puppet president during the Trujillo dictatorship, was inaugurated the same year. Thereafter, he was reelected for two consecutive terms, extending his period in office until 1978—a period commonly known in Dominican politics as *los doce años de Balaguer* (Balaguer's twelve years).

Under the Balaguer presidency, Haitian-Dominican relations took a new turn. Balaguer had previously (1947)—and openly—professed during his career an intensive anti-Haitian prejudice, coupled with a strong nationalist zeal, but he also was a pragmatic politician, with vast experience in public affairs acquired during the Trujillo years. Balaguer clearly understood the practicality of reestablishing diplomatic relations with Haiti. Based on these common needs, Haiti and the Dominican Republic resumed diplomatic relations in 1966 (Black 1986, 121). Relations between both countries during Balaguer's twelve years were correct, if not cordial.

Balaguer and Duvalier also shared another interest: regulating the importation of Haitian cane-cutters for the Dominican sugar harvest. The Duvalier administration made huge profits from this practice, while the Dominican government was provided with a stable and guaranteed source of cheap laborers, at a time when sugar was still the mainstay of the Dominican economy. According to the 1966 agreement, part of the workers' salary was retained and given to the Haitian government as a savings fund, to be returned to the workers upon their arrival in Haiti. The Haitian government never gave the money back to the workers (Lundahl 1979, 346).

When François Duvalier died in 1971, his son, Jean-Claude "Baby Doc" Duvalier, inherited the presidency-for-life in a smooth transition of power. Jean-Claude surrounded himself with a coterie of technocrats, a fact reflected in his foreign policy. In an effort to create a humane facade for his dictatorship and develop Haiti's economy, Baby Doc sought to attract foreign investment. In 1972, he signed an agreement with the Balaguer administration to establish a joint free trade zone, reduce tariffs, simplify trade transactions, and improve transportation between both countries (Black 1986, 121).

The PRD and Haiti

Balaguer's defeat in the 1978 elections paved the way for a democratic opening in Dominican politics. Although the transition was not without problems (a faction of the Dominican military tried to stage a coup to keep Balaguer in office), it was the first time in the contemporary period that an opposition party took power in the Dominican Republic. The opposition's candidate, Antonio Guzmán of the PRD (Bosch's former party), was elected by a clear margin. Guzmán not only inaugurated a new era in Dominican politics but sought to improve relations with Haiti. He concentrated on expanding trade between Haiti and the Dominican Republic, and on reducing their traditional cultural and racial antagonisms (Wiarda and Kryzanek 1992, 139). Guzmán and Jean-Claude Duvalier met in 1979 and then later the same year to inaugurate a joint irrigation project. A similar approach was followed by Guzmán's PRD successor, Salvador Jorge Blanco, who won the 1982 elections.

Unfortunately, and in spite of their liberal, social democratic rhetoric, the PRD administrations did little to alleviate the plight of Haitian *braceros* (cane-cutters) in the Dominican Republic. Low sugar prices, combined with the unwillingness of the Dominican government to accept Duvalier's contract terms, meant that for some years the sugar harvest had to be carried out without contract workers. The government then resorted to the use of *amba fil* (illegal) workers.[2] When the amba fils proved not to be enough, the Consejo Estatal del Azúcar (CEA), the government's sugar corporation, resorted to the forced "recruitment" (that is, roundups and forced relocations) of Haitians living in the Dominican Republic, regardless of their legal status.

The Dominican military, in charge of the operation, developed a highly profitable traffic of forced laborers, a situation denounced in international forums by the International Labor Organization (ILO) and the Anti-Slavery Society (Plant 1987, chap. 6). Haitians, or any black-skinned males who could not conclusively prove that they were Dominican, were rounded up in coffee farms, small villages, road checkpoints, and even in the capital city of Santo Domingo. They were then taken, under the cover of night, to the CEA's sugar mills or "sold" to private sugar mills (Plant 1987, 74–84; Veras 1983, 62–63). Antihaitianismo ideology once again played an important role, as few voices of dissent were heard among Dominican politicians and public opinion makers.

The fall of the Duvalier dictatorship on 7 February 1986 ended the practice of bilateral accords and created an urgent problem for the Dominican sugar industry. Two million dollars had been paid to the Duvalier administration at the end of 1985, as part of that year's accord. The rapidly deteriorating situation in Haiti, however, precluded the recruitment of any braceros by the Haitian authorities. After the fall of Duvalier, the CEA found itself with no money, no braceros, and a worthless contract (Plant 1987, 88). Again, the CEA and the Dominican military resorted to the large-scale roundup of "Haitians."

The Return of Balaguer

Nineteen eighty-six was a transcendental year in Hispaniola. Sparked by massive popular protest in the interior that spread to the capital, the Duvalier dictatorship collapsed. The army remained indifferent, and Duvalier was "convinced" by friendly nations (the United States, France, and Canada) to leave. Besides the fall of the Duvalier dictatorship in Haiti, the Dominican people witnessed the unimaginable: Joaquín Balaguer, nearly blind, eighty years old, and discarded by the opposition as a viable candidate, won a fifth presidential term. Even more inconceivable was that in 1990 he was reelected for a sixth term with a margin of fewer than 25,000 votes (D'Agostino 1992). The scandalous graft and corruption of the two PRD administrations, combined with a deep economic crisis and the mellowing effects of time, made los doce años de Balaguer look rather rosy for many Dominicans.

After the fall of Jean-Claude Duvalier, Haiti entered into a period of social and political instability as different groups competed for power. Among these groups were the military, the former Duvalierists, popular organizations, low-ranking church officials (ti legliz), and exiles who had returned after Duvalier's fall (Abbott 1991; Wilentz 1989). During the period from 1986 to 1991, Haiti had several de facto governments, including two headed by army commanders, Henri Namphy and Prosper Avril, who ruled by decree.

Balaguer adopted a cautious diplomatic approach during that turbulent period, for he feared that events in Haiti would have negative consequences for the Dominican Republic. Severe civil unrest in Haiti could provoke a flood of Haitian refugees fleeing into the Dominican Republic, a nightmarish situation that the Dominican government was not prepared to handle. Balaguer maintained correct relations with the different Haitian administrations in turn, and even granted asylum to several Haitian leaders after they were overthrown. For example, General and President-de-facto Henri Namphy, overthrown on 17 September 1988, was flown with his family to the Dominican Republic, where they still reside (Wilentz 1989, 359).

The election of Father Jean-Bertrand Aristide in 1990 created a public relations problem for the Balaguer administration. Aristide, inaugurated on 7 February 1991 (five years after Duvalier's fall), was an outspoken leader for the Haitian lower classes. A devout follower of liberation theology, Aristide, and his Lavalas movement,[3] sought to profoundly transform Haitian society. He also openly denounced in international forums (like the United Nations) the slavelike working conditions of Haitians in the Dominican Republic.

These accusations came in the midst of a wave of reports from human rights organizations (such as Americas Watch), U.S. television news, and the ILO, in which the Dominican Republic was depicted as a human rights violator. To make matters worse, the U.S. trade representative decided to review these allegations before certifying the Dominican Republic as eligible for the U.S. Generalized System of Preferences (GSP) (Ferguson 1992, 87–88). An unfavorable decision would have certainly meant economic disaster for the Dominican Republic, as the GSP guarantees preferential access to the U.S. market. Not surprisingly, Aristide became a persona non grata for the Balaguer administration, as well as for most of the Dominican economic elites. Once gain, antihaitianismo ideology flourished as the old anti-Haitian discourse was revived.

Aristide was the target of personal defamatory attacks, in a concerted effort to destroy his credibility. Even opposition politicians, such as Jacobo Majluta (a wealthy businessman and former PRD presidential candidate), joined the anti-Haitian campaign and launched vicious attacks against Aristide:

Jean-Bertrand did not attack President Joaquín Balaguer; "he went to the international forums to harshly attack the Dominican Republic."

On the day of his [Aristide's] inauguration "he took along a witch and walked the Bishop of that nation through the streets of Port-au-Prince in a shameful manner and committed anti-democratic acts."

He [Aristide] accused us [the Dominican Republic] in front of the OAS, ILO and the UN [United Nations] of all the evils of the world (Sarita 1993, 4).

Fabio Herrera Cabral, undersecretary of foreign relations of the Balaguer administration, warned that "Dominicans must be ready to counter any intrusion that he [Aristide] pretends in order to impose his ideas on the Dominican Republic" (Carvajal 1993, 16).

Balaguer responded to Aristide's accusations with decree 233–91. The decree ordered the immediate deportation of all illegal Haitians under the age of sixteen or over sixty. Within three months, about 50,000 Haitians were deported (Ferguson 1992, 89). The Dominican military profited from this operation by confiscating the possessions of deported Haitians. The deportation decree was clearly aimed at destabilizing the Aristide administration, and on 30 September 1991, Aristide was overthrown by a military coup led by General Raoul Cédras.

The Balaguer administration did not condemn the coup against Aristide. To the contrary, for days after the coup, the Dominican press was saturated with opinion articles condemning Aristide and blaming his unstable character for the coup that toppled his administration (Cuello 1991). Other articles remarked that Haiti was a highly unstable country, practically ungovernable, and that it was thus condemned to be ruled by strongmen. Antihaitianismo ideology was conveniently reversed to "blame the victim": the Haitian people, and Aristide in particular, were guilty of Haiti's misfortunes. Moreover, the Dominican Republic was portrayed as foreign to these problems, and simply defending itself from baseless, unprovoked, and mean-spirited accusations.

Though the Balaguer administration had publicly offered to help resolve the Haitian impasse and had officially supported the OAS/UN embargo against the Haitian military government, it took actions to prevent, or at least delay, the resolution of the Haitian crisis. In 1993, the Balaguer administration authorized the sale of foodstuffs and fuel to Haiti for "humanitarian reasons" (M. M. Pérez 1993, 1, 16). Later, when the embargo was tightened, and in a clear violation of OAS/UN-imposed sanctions, all sorts of goods—but mainly gasoline—were carried over the border and into Haiti, in full view of the Dominican military, which profited enormously from this contraband (French 1994b). In conclusion, the international embargo was as strong as its weakest link—the Dominican Republic.

Antihaitianismo ideology has not been an overt principle of Dominican foreign policy. This was the case during the 1963 crisis and again during the Balaguer-Aristide confrontation. Though Balaguer rallied anti-Haitian nationalism during the Aristide "crisis" and employed antihaitianismo's legitimizing discourse, the whole affair was clearly an astute political move designed to bolster his domestic support, as even his political opponents supported Balaguer's position. Antihaitianismo ideology, ostensibly targeting the foreign "other," is really designed for domestic consumption and control. The use of a foreign element (Haiti/Aristide) was simply an expedient (and temporary) factor employed for domestic political purposes. For example, right after the ouster of Aristide, Balaguer established "normal"— in spite of the embargo—relations with the Haitian military junta.

While antihaitianismo has played a discrete or subliminal role in Dominican foreign policy, it has played an influential and open role in Dominican domestic politics. The continued importance of antihaitianismo ideology was made poignantly clear during the 1994 and 1996 elections.

Antihaitianismo in the 1994 Elections

This book has shown the value of antihaitianismo ideology as a powerful political weapon. Never was this fact more evident than during the 1994 elections in the Dominican Republic. On one hand, the full impact of the Haitian crisis happened to coincide with the May 1994 elections. The return of Aristide to Haiti seemed imminent, for he had the full backing of the international community and mainly of U.S. president Bill Clinton, who was committed to the restoration of democracy in Haiti. And on the other, a black man of presumed Haitian ancestry, José Francisco Peña Gómez of the PRD, was the front-runner in the Dominican electoral campaign against the perennial electoral caudillo, Joaquín Balaguer. The 1994 campaign is a perfect example of the use of antihaitianismo ideology as a political weapon, particularly in a negative advertisement campaign designed to undermine Peña Gómez's lead. Most of the "mudslinging" strategies employed had been developed in the United States and were simply adapted to the Dominican political context, where they proved to be extremely successful.

On 16 May 1994, the Dominican Republic held national elections. Amid strong allegations of fraud, Joaquín Balaguer of the Partido Reformista Social Cristiano (PRSC, formerly PR) became president of the Dominican Republic for the seventh time in his life, defeating his opponents by a scant margin of 22,281 votes.[4] Balaguer's premier position in the Dominican political system has not gone unchallenged, but he has rarely been defeated (only in 1978 and 1982). Through adroit maneuvering, co-optation, or repression, Balaguer has always been able to defeat his enemies or win them to his side (Kryzanek 1978). The 1994 elections presented a new challenge for the then-eighty-seven-year-old Balaguer, though. Physically frail and blind, Balaguer sought reelection for a third consecutive term, against the strong opposition of Peña Gómez and the PRD.

As the leading presidential candidate in most opinion polls (Vega 1994b), Peña Gómez was the main target of his opponents' campaign strategists. Negative advertising was nothing new in Dominican politics. Personal defamatory attacks are employed—and expected—by all candidates. For example, Joaquín Balaguer was the target of attacks for his old age and visual problems. Juan Bosch's mental health has often been questioned (he was eighty-four years old for the 1994 elections), and he has been portrayed as an atheist and a radical leftist. But Peña Gómez was particularly vulnerable to negative advertising for reasons having more to do with the Dominican Republic's social structures and dominant culture than with Peña Gómez himself.

Peña Gómez came from a humble background. An orphan whose parents had to flee for their lives during the 1937 massacre, he rose from poverty and obscurity to the national spotlight through his own efforts. As commendable as that successful struggle may be, in the Dominican political system it can become a handicap. Both politics and the military have been avenues of vertical mobility for middle-and lower-class Dominicans, but traditionally, high-level Dominican politics has been the game of the powerful and prestigious. Elite family cliques, with strong business interests, exercise a powerful influence on the political decision-making process.

The Dominican elite is a small group connected by marriage, business, family, and friendship (Rosario 1992). Class discrimination is one of the most powerful prejudices in Dominican society. In a recent survey, class prejudices were mentioned as the main cause of the lack of equal opportunities in the country (75.3 percent of respondents)—with racial discrimination following in second place (44.5 percent of respondents) (Duarte and others 1995, 16).

Given his lower-class origins, Peña Gómez did not fit the elites' traditional mold. To them, he was an "outsider" and the poor man's candidate, opposed to conservative interests. As he did not belong—and had no connections to—the traditional elite families, his candidacy was seen with apprehension by some members of the elites, who preferred a candidate more amenable to their taste. Even though he was one of the country's top political leaders, his black color still tied him to his lower-class origins (in the eyes of the elites, who are mostly light-skinned).

So not only was Peña Gómez a lower-class candidate (with no elite family ties) aspiring to national power, but he was also a *black* lower-class candidate.[5] Racial prejudice is not as rampant in the Dominican Republic as in South Africa, the United States, or even neighboring Cuba. As we have seen, a person is not considered black just because he or she is not purely white. Prejudice in the Dominican Republic is subtle, sometimes unnoticeable, but it has a powerful influence on Dominican society.

Peña Gómez was, however, even by the loose Dominican racial standards, a pure black; that is, he had dark skin and no "fine" features, making his acceptance into light-skinned circles more difficult. Furthermore, he was not a musician or a baseball player but a presidential candidate, aspiring to the highest office in the nation, and with a good chance of winning. These characteristics made Peña Gómez a very threatening figure for his political opponents.

Peña Gómez was also accused of being of Haitian origin—which made him an enemy of the Dominican people and a threat to the Dominican nationhood. According to his political enemies, he was a fifth columnist with a hidden agenda who secretly wished to reunify Haiti and the Dominican Republic. Not surprisingly, the attitude of some Dominicans toward Peña Gómez was a reflection of popular attitudes toward Haiti: fear, hatred, and distrust. In a 1985 political survey, 24.03 percent of the respondents mentioned that the Haitian ancestry of Peña Gómez was his main obstacle as a presidential candidate, while another 5.85 percent mentioned Peña Gómez's black skin color—and the fact that the Dominican Republic is a racist country—as his main political obstacle (Álvarez Vega 1985, 35).

The presumed Haitian origins of Peña Gómez led his enemies to question even his Catholic beliefs, in addition to his loyalty to the Dominican Republic. In another words, his dominicanidad (Dominicanness) was questioned. This "us against foreigners" strategy (Johnson-Cartee and Copeland 1991, 113) centered on two issues: Peña Gómez's supposed voodoo beliefs and his hidden loyalty to Haiti.

The voodoo campaign was the result of a video shot years earlier, when Peña Gómez attended a healing ceremony conducted by Brazilian psychic healer Ivan Trihla. The video caused a commotion in the Dominican Republic, where it was presented by the Fuerza Nacional Progresista (National Progressive Force, or FNP; an ally of the Partido de la Liberación Dominicana [Dominican Liberation Party, or PLD]) as unequivocal proof that Peña Gómez was a voodoo-practicing Haitian who believed in satanic rites. The original video clip was edited with the addition of music and voice-overs, so as to give it a more somber aspect. Several versions of this negative political advertisement were aired. One shows Trihla dedicating the ceremony to "my friend" Peña Gómez. Another version focuses on the different satanic aspects of the ceremony—such as spiritual possession—and ends with a shot of Peña Gómez, barefoot, trembling, and brushing off his body with his hands, as if he were being possessed by a spirit.[6] An anonymous fax pictures Peña Gómez during the ceremony in a deep trance, invoking the infernal spirits in order to achieve power in the Dominican Republic. In the background, there is the silhouette of a girl hugging her mother, with the caption, "Mommy . . . I am scared."

Peña Gómez's enemies also spread rumors that he wanted to unify the two nations (Haiti and the Dominican Republic), that he would avenge the 1937 massacre, that he would allow thousands of Haitian migrants into the country, that the Haitian government supported him, and so forth. These charges were nothing new; this defamatory campaign against Peña Gómez had been going on for years. However, Peña Gómez's strong lead in the polls during the 1994 electoral campaign added a new urgency to the mud-slinging campaign, bringing it to the center of the Dominican political stage.

This popularity also made Peña Gómez the main obstacle to Balaguer's reelection plans. Balaguer is well known for his anti-Haitian, nationalist postures, and he had the savvy to rally anti-Haitian nationalism among the Dominican people. *La problemática haitiana* (the Haitian problem) touches deep chords in the Dominican popular psyche, and as such, it can be a trump card in the Dominican political system. Peña Gómez's opponents played that card very well.

Weeks before the 1994 elections, a flier—supposedly written (in Creole) by a Haitian group—supporting Peña Gómez was sent to fax machines throughout the Dominican Republic. In another anonymous fax, Peña Gómez is pictured torturing Vincho Castillo (of the FNP) and Lidio Cadet (of the PLD) "Haitian-style," that is, with car tires around their necks. In yet another fax, Peña Gómez has a whip in one hand and a torch in the other, in the process of setting the Dominican Republic on fire. Two other faxes picture Peña Gómez and Balaguer competing against each other in boxing and baseball: Balaguer, representing the Dominican Republic, knocks out Peña Gómez (representing Haiti) with a demolishing upper cut, while pitcher Balaguer strikes out Peña Gómez, who wears a Haitian uniform. In another fax, Peña Gómez tries to cast his vote when someone standing in line complains, "Hey, hey, that one is not Dominican!" The official at the electoral table stops Peña Gómez and asks him to say *perejil* (a difficult word for a Francophone speaker to pronounce).[7] Appendix C contains examples of the anti-Peña Gómez, anti-Haitian fax campaign.

Television ads were equally vicious. Appeals to nationalism and the use of patriotic symbols predominated. For example, one PRSC ad warns Dominicans not to follow those who want to unify the island. In a masterful use of subliminal messages, the ad shows a map of the island, with Haiti in brown (representing erosion) and the Dominican Republic in green. However, the map has something strange about it. It is a map of the island from 1777, when the French and the Spanish established the first formal border (see map 1). That map presents a Dominican Republic (then Santo Domingo) that is larger than today's, as Haiti later annexed territories to the east during its revolution. In the course of the ad, a brown tide takes over the whole island, and the part belonging to the Dominican Republic shatters into pieces. A voice-over, accompanied by a musical jingle, warns, "Because our sovereignty is in danger."

Another ad presents the PRSC's vice presidential candidate, Jacinto Peynado, making a personal appeal to the opposition to support President Balaguer, because that is the only way to "defend our sovereignty." These remarks followed a statement made by Balaguer early in the campaign, when he denounced a supposed plan by "powerful countries" (a reference to the United States and Western Europe) to solve the Haitian crisis by unifying the island.

Other anti-Haitian television ads appealed to the lower classes by using jingles with simple lyrics, compelling musical scores, and powerful symbolic images. One of those jingles (produced by the PRSC) asks, "What is it that those people want? Oh, oh, that we speak patois [Creole]!" The ad then shows a huge black hand taking over a map of the Dominican Republic. Another television ad depicts a group of PRSC leaders embracing each other in a display of unity "because our sovereignty is in danger." The ad goes on to show a group of schoolchildren about to raise the flag, but the one they have in their hands is a folded Haitian flag (shown for just a second). When the flag is finally raised, the ad shows a Dominican flag.

These constant references to "our sovereignty [which is] in danger" were clear attacks against Peña Gómez, who was constantly accused by his enemies of having a Haitian "hidden agenda," that is, a secret plan to reunify the island. A pamphlet published before the electoral campaign warned Dominicans that Peña Gómez was the political reincarnation of Jean-Jacques Dessalines and that he sought power in order to vindicate Haiti's claim to the whole island (R. D. Jiménez 1993). Balaguer even justified his authoritarian style during the campaign by stating that he was "a Dominican president who feels for the Dominican Republic."

Finally, early in the morning of election day (16 May 1994), the rumor that the United States had just invaded Haiti was spread among the thousands of voters waiting in line. Even after the elections, the attacks continued as Peña Gómez questioned the integrity of the voting process and accused the PRSC of committing "massive" fraud.[8] Soon, a video appeared showing Haitians who had been issued Dominican voter registration cards and who unabashedly proclaimed that they had voted for "their candidate" Peña Gómez. This vicious anti-Haitian campaign against Peña Gómez was aptly described by Dominican historian Frank Moya Pons as "the worst display of racism that we have seen since the Haitian-Dominican wars" (French 1994b).

Balaguer once again played the ultranationalist, anti-Haitian card. He was portrayed by his followers as the defender of the Dominican nation against an international conspiracy to unite the two nations (French 1994a). Not surprisingly, a survey conducted during the electoral campaign showed that 30 percent of Dominicans considered that the color and race of a candidate were important ("Fusión" 1994, 34). While this Haitian-bashing campaign was taking place, relations with the de facto regime in Haiti remained normal. After the elections, Balaguer finally agreed to let an international force of observers help the Dominican military enforce the embargo. Immediately thereafter, the Clinton administration recognized Balaguer's victory, and even the new U.S. ambassador in Santo Domingo attended the inaugural ceremony.

Antihaitianismo in the 1996 Election

The 1996 presidential election was held as the result of the grave irregularities that took place during the 1994 elections (Sagás 1997). After months of postelectoral crisis, representatives of the PLD, PRD, and PRSC signed a political agreement on 10 August 1994, which called for a new presidential election in 1996 and important modifications to the Dominican constitution. Holding the post of president for consecutive terms was banned (which prevented Balaguer from running as a candidate in 1996), and a two-round electoral system was designed.[9] Besides the absence of Balaguer, the 1996 presidential election was characterized by the absence of Juan Bosch. Bosch, the perennial presidential candidate of the PLD, retired from politics shortly after the 1994 elections, and Leonel Fernández, a young lawyer and Bosch's running mate in 1994, was selected as the PLD's presidential candidate for 1996. Vice President Jacinto Peynado was the presidential candidate on the PRSC ticket.

The 1996 electoral campaign witnessed a repetition of the "dirty campaign" against Peña Gómez, though in a less intense fashion. The difference may be explained by the fact that Balaguer was not a candidate this time, and that he showed very little interest in supporting Peynado. Instead, Balaguer remained aloof throughout most of the campaign and even failed to show up to vote on 16 May 1996. Most of the negative ads were run instead by Vincho Castillo and the PLD. The issues were the same: Peña Gómez was a "Haitian" with the secret agenda of unifying the two countries; powerful nations were making plans to use the Dominican Republic as a dumping ground for Haitian refugees; and Haitians would illegally vote for "their candidate" Peña Gómez.

Just two weeks before the election, Leonel Fernández declared that as many as 25 percent of registered voters were Haitian nationals. The PRD replied with allegations that the PLD had plans to try to prevent blacks from voting. The PRD even published newspaper ads asking blacks not to be intimidated and to go and vote.[10] In spite of the mudslinging campaign, Peña Gómez remained well ahead in the polls and easily won the election with 45.93 percent of the votes, but he fell short of the required 50 percent. Leonel Fernández came in second with 38.94 percent. A run-off election was scheduled for 30 June 1996.

On 2 June 1996, the anti-Peña Gómez campaign was consolidated with the creation of the Frente Patriótico Nacional (National Patriotic Front), an electoral alliance between the PLD and the PRSC (and their allies) masterminded by Balaguer. According to Balaguer, his party would "unselfishly" support Leonel Fernández in the run-off election to save Dominican sovereignty from falling into "not truly Dominican" hands (an obvious reference to Peña Gómez), and just for the satisfaction of "remaining a Dominican on Dominican soil" (M. Jiménez 1996). In reality, Balaguer had made a skillful political move (with the complicity of the PLD leadership). Not only had he practically ensured Peña Gómez's defeat, but he had also chosen to support a young, inexperienced candidate whose party had a tiny minority in Congress (and thus presented no threat to him).[11]

The Unión Nacionalista (Nationalist Union), a conservative organization, followed suit by accusing Peña Gómez of planning to turn the Dominican Republic into a refuge for the Haitian diaspora, and called upon Dominicans to make a "patriotic decision" and vote against him. The anti-Haitian alliance sealed the fate of Peña Gómez, who labeled it "racist" and "antipopular." With the combined votes of the PLD and his PRSC supporters, Leonel Fernández won the second round with 51.25 percent of the votes.

In a bitter postelection speech, Peña Gómez declared that racism had played an important role in his electoral defeat. Racism, he confessed, was well entrenched in Dominican society, and had he been elected president, a bloodbath would have taken place. He finished by remarking that "Dominican society is not yet ready for a black president" (M.A. Núñez 1996). Peña Gómez died on 10 May 1998 without realizing his lifelong dream.

Did Antihaitianismo's "Dirty Campaigns" Work?

Of all the candidates during the 1994 and 1996 electoral races in the Dominican Republic, José Francisco Peña Gómez was the most vulnerable to negative advertising. And the fact that he led in most opinion polls throughout the races only brought more relentless attacks against his person. Anti-Haitian mudslinging certainly took votes away from Peña Gómez. Whether it made the difference during the 1994 elections is hard to establish. But in an election where the official margin of victory was only 22,281 votes (out of a total of 3 million votes that were cast), it definitely played an important role. In 1996, the Frente Patriótico Nacional, an anti–Peña Gómez, anti-

Haitian electoral alliance, certainly provided the edge that Leonel Fernández needed for his victory.

Still, the fact that more than 1.2 million Dominicans voted for Peña Gómez in 1994—and again in 1996—was an indication of his strong popularity among the electorate, considering all the odds against him.[12] It has been argued that political ads do not transform attitudes overnight, "but can play a 'supplementary' role by aiding a segment of the electorate, especially weak partisan identifiers, independents, apoliticals, poorly-informed voters, and late deciders in obtaining information and knowledge about campaign issues and candidates" (Lee 1991, 24). Mudslinging in the Dominican Republic seems to have the greatest impact on the undecided voters, that is, those who make up their minds on the last days before elections. In the past, most of the seemingly undecided had voted for Balaguer, that is, about 10–11 percent of the electorate (Penn 1986, 8). They were the target of negative advertising, the idea being that they would vote conservatively, for the "known" (that is, Balaguer). Furthermore, negative political advertising had a powerful agenda-setting function during the 1994 and 1996 electoral campaigns. In pivotal elections, where candidates should have concentrated on issues of great concern to the country's future—the cost of living, unemployment, et cetera—the candidates' image prevailed over the issues.[13]

The anti-Haitian mudslinging campaign also hurt Peña Gómez personally and limited his political discourse. Although his supporters claimed that Peña Gómez was used to this character defamation campaign and was not affected by it, others claimed that these attacks had left their mark on Peña Gómez's personality. A well-publicized psychological profile of the main candidates, published one month before the 1994 elections, described Peña Gómez as a man traumatized by his childhood tragedy (his parents had run away to Haiti during the 1937 massacre, abandoning him and his sister) and full of racial complexes (Rosario Adames 1994). Moreover, Peña Gómez had been so closely identified with Haiti by his opponents that his campaign strategists advised him to refrain from debating about Haiti, and even to avoid using the words *Haiti* and *Haitians* (Vásquez 1994). This step was taken to avoid falling into a rhetorical trap and to avoid being quoted out of context.

Finally, in an election mired in charges of fraud, mudslinging helped to further distract public opinion during the 1994 postelectoral crisis. What began as a national issue very soon took on an international dimension. The outrage of the international community (including the U.S. Department of State, members of the U.S. Congress, foreign heads of state, international observers, the international news media, and private and public organizations) over the tainted 1994 electoral process was skillfully distorted into "foreign interference" through a negative advertising campaign. The refusal of the Balaguer administration to comply with the embargo against Haiti was transformed into "a defense of our sovereignty" in the media. When the opposition and the international community demanded satisfactory answers from the Dominican government, the response was a flag-waving campaign, in which "real Dominicans" were asked to display the Dominican flag outside their homes in a gesture of national solidarity against those who wanted to impose foreign solutions on the Dominican people.[14] In this fashion, the anti-Haitian mudslinging campaign, by its "distractiveness," helped defuse a potentially explosive political situation in Balaguer's favor.

Furthermore, the negative image that had been built around Peña Gómez robbed him of much-needed support. While he seemed to have ample international support, in the national political arena he faced the opposition of not only the PRSC but also the PLD. It must be kept in mind that some of the most virulent negative ads were produced by the FNP, an ally of the PLD. The PLD apparently had not forgotten the PRD's lack of support for the PLD's allegations of fraud during the 1990 elections, when Balaguer defeated Bosch, also by a narrow margin. These "divide and conquer" tactics proved to be extremely effective for the PRSC, which has always won whenever the political opposition is divided. Moreover, the PRSC-PLD unspoken (and later official) "anti–Peña Gómez alliance" effectively turned the PRD into a minority party in the Dominican Congress after the 1994 elections and robbed it of a seemingly imminent victory during the 1996 election.

In conclusion, anti-Haitian negative political advertising, or mudslinging, as distracting and morally reproachable as it may be, unfortunately worked very well. In a country like the Dominican Republic, with high indexes of illiteracy and poverty, an authoritarian political culture, underlying racial and social strains, and a history of animosity toward Haiti, mudslinging against PRD presidential candidate José Francisco Peña Gómez was deadly. Anti–Peña Gómez ads took votes away from the PRD by convincing undecided or apolitical voters to vote for the PRSC, the PLD, or not to vote at all. It also propagated a negative public image of Peña Gómez as an irrational, unstable, superstitious, and pro-Haitian candidate. In an election under the shadow of the Haitian crisis (in 1994), anti–Peña Gómez mudslinging allowed Balaguer to manipulate the international crisis to his domestic advantage, and to hold on to power for two more years. Negative political advertising against Peña Gómez robbed the PRD of vital domestic support during the 1994 campaign and the subsequent postelectoral crisis. In an election marred by charges of widespread fraud, this lack of domestic political support weakened the PRD's case. Later, in an election in which he was not even a candidate at all (in 1996), Balaguer played a central role by reviving anti-Haitian nationalism and using his political leverage once again to prevent Peña Gómez from becoming president. Negative political advertising in the Dominican Republic has proven to be an excellent political weapon, one that rarely fails or backfires.

Antihaitianismo ideology, thought by some to be on the decline, seems to have been just dormant. It was revived during the 1994 and 1996 elections, when Peña Gómez had a clear lead in the polls. Indeed, antihaitianismo ideology, as expressed through an anti–Peña Gómez, anti-Haitian mudslinging campaign, played a central role in both electoral campaigns. Millions of pesos were spent by Peña Gómez's opponents in a barrage of print and broadcast ads. And in 1996, Bosch and Balaguer, two eternal opponents, joined forces in the creation of an electoral alliance openly based on racist, anti-Haitian, and ultranationalist principles. Moreover, once again antihaitianismo ideology divided the Dominican people (particularly the lower classes) not only according to their position on politics and "the Haitian issue" but also by their color. Blackness was identified with political sympathy for Peña Gómez and—by extension—with Haiti. Prejudice and discrimination, thought to be nonexistent in a racially mixed society, again pitted Dominicans against each other. Unfortunately, it still seems that, at least in the Dominican political arena, antihaitianismo ideology is far from dead.

Conclusion

Antihaitianismo ideology suits both the foreign and domestic political goals of the Dominican elites. In the "foreign" arena, antihaitianismo ideology accounts for an ultranationalist discourse that does not correspond with the collusive nature of diplomatic relations between Haiti and the Dominican Republic—particularly regarding Dominican support for authoritarian regimes in Haiti. In the domestic arena, antihaitianismo ideology remains entrenched as a visible component of Dominican domestic politics. This fact underscores the real nature of antihaitianismo ideology and partly explains its political resilience. Rather than a foreign policy directive, antihaitianismo ideology is really a domestic political tool, geared toward the maintenance of an inequitable social order and the preservation of elite privileges. Masterful in its use of political disguise, antihaitianismo ideology confuses the foreign and domestic political realms in its ultranationalist discourse, just as it confuses race, nation, and ethnicity. Thus antihaitianismo ideology has a Janus face: seemingly foreign issues are really domestic, while domestic issues have a foreign nexus. This foreign-domestic link is an element of continuity in the long and intricate history of antihaitianismo ideology in the Dominican Republic.

Conclusion

The Political Manipulation of Race

This book has examined the creation, development, diffusion, and political uses of antihaitianismo ideology in the Dominican Republic. Still, there are some lingering questions, which will be addressed here. First, is antihaitianismo a full-fledged ideology or just a loose concoction of ideas? Second, is antihaitianismo ideology unique, or is it just a local version of racist ideologies? Third, what are the consequences of the persistence of antihaitianismo in the Dominican Republic? And fourth, what implications does the Dominican case have for the study of ethnic and/or racial conflict elsewhere?

Is Antihaitianismo a "Real" Ideology?

In the nineteenth and twentieth centuries, antihaitianismo went through a series of stages, and its intensity varied, depending on historical circumstances. From a high in the years after Dominican independence, anti-Haitian sentiment declined toward the end of the nineteenth century but did not disappear. After the U.S. occupation of Haiti and the Dominican Republic, relations between the latter two countries were described as "correct." It was not until the years after the 1937 massacre that antihaitianismo ideology reached its zenith.

Probably the only moment in Dominican history when antihaitianismo could be classified as a state-sponsored ideology was during the Trujillo era. Wiarda (1968) examined in detail the Trujillo dictatorship and concluded that, under certain conditions, the Trujillo dictatorship did fit the totalitarian model. Totalitarian regimes require an ideology, and Trujillo's regime had one. But even others who disagree with the totalitarian label have also stressed the importance of ideology for the Trujillo regime (Hartlyn 1998b).

Although Trujillo was a Trujillista first and foremost, he is also considered a nationalist. He cultivated Dominican intellectuals and made them the ideologues of his regime. These intellectuals, such as Joaquín Balaguer and Manuel A. Peña Batlle, developed a nationalist, Catholic, Hispanic, anti-Haitian, and anticommunist state ideology (F. J. Franco 1973, 100–103). They molded antihaitianismo into a coherent, if weakly based, state ideology (from an intellectual standpoint). In their discourse, not only did Haitians represent the opposite of everything Dominican; Haiti and Haitian migrants were considered an imminent threat to the nation's survival as a cultural entity. This grave danger demanded radical solutions and a strong leadership, which only Trujillo could provide. Trujillo's propaganda machine drilled these tenets into the minds of Dominicans. For thirty-one years, generations of Dominicans were taught these ideas as unquestionable principles.

The sponsorship of antihaitianismo by the Dominican Trujillista state marked the highest point in its long evolution and equated antihaitianismo with other racist ideologies in more developed nations, such as Nazism in Germany and Apartheid in South Africa. Antihaitianismo, and the myths related to it, were a major source of legitimacy for the Trujillo dictatorship, thus helping to institutionalize it. As Andrés L. Mateo argues, "The discursive symbolism of the Trujillista regime magically inhabited the totality of the citizen's life" (1993, 14). Antihaitianismo ideology even defended the undefendable: the 1937 massacre, concealing its repercussions under a mantle of myths and lies.

After the fall of Trujillo, antihaitianismo did not disappear, though it was no longer a state-sponsored ideology. Many of the intellectuals who formulated it—especially Balaguer—went on to occupy important political posts, from which they kept reproducing their prejudiced discourse.

Since 1961, antihaitianismo has remained a political tool. Yet events like the election of Juan Bosch in 1962, the 1965 civil war, the spread of liberal and leftist ideas in the Dominican Republic, and the migration of thousands of Dominicans to the United States (where many of them "learned" for the first time that they were black) have undermined its appeal. Contesting ideologies, which were subdued by the coercive power of the Trujillista state, now challenge official "truths." Dominicans no longer unconditionally accept the state's propaganda. Nevertheless, antihaitianismo remains a powerful dominant ideology to this day.[1]

Antihaitianismo has had a long and intricate evolution. From its origins as Hispanic racism, to its transformation into anti-Haitian nationalism, to its culmination as Trujillo's state ideology, antihaitianismo has had one main objective: the protection of powerful personal and elite interests through the subjugation of the lower (and darker) sectors of the Dominican population. Antihaitianismo serves Dominican elite interests well and has even been accepted by the great majority of the Dominican people as part of the political culture, thereby institutionalizing it and giving it legitimacy.

Prejudice and racism—as expressed through antihaitianismo ideology—distract attention from class and economic issues. For example, in the middle of an economic crisis and an acute scarcity of basic foodstuffs, informal trade with Haiti was deemed the culprit. When Balaguer seemed on the verge of being defeated by Peña Gómez during the 1994 electoral campaign, he framed the race as a struggle for the survival of Dominican sovereignty in the face of an international conspiracy bent on forcefully uniting Haiti and the Dominican Republic into a single nation. If observers point to the unemployment problem in the Dominican Republic, it is argued that illegal Haitian migrants steal jobs and lower wages. Hence antihaitianismo ideology is a useful "smoke and mirrors" tactic for the dominant classes.

Is Antihaitianismo Unique?

Cuban, Dominican, and Puerto Rican intellectuals interpreted their "national problem" in similar ways. For Cuban intellectuals like José Antonio Saco, Francisco Figueras, and Fernando Ortiz Fernández, race was central to the "national problem." Saco, who died in 1879 (before slavery was abolished in Cuba), promoted abolition to stop the inflow of blacks into Cuba. After abolition was accomplished, miscegenation and massive white immigration could "whiten" the Cuban people (Martínez-Fernández 1994, 140). For Figueras, Cubans, given their mixed racial composition, were incapable of forming an independent republic. Climate and environment also contributed to their decay. For Ortiz, blacks lacked civilization and morals, and they were a source of crime, too (Helg 1990, 39, 47–53). Most of the solutions proposed to the Cuban elites' dilemma involved the elimination of black cultural influences, closer ties with "civilized" nations (mainly the United States), and white immigration.

In Puerto Rico, the "national problem" was phrased in similar terms by Antonio S. Pedreira in *Insularismo: Ensayos de interpretación puertorriqueña*. Published in 1934, *Insularismo* represented the vision of the Puerto Rican people held by its elites. Lower-class Puerto Rican peasants (or jíbaros) were considered docile, ignorant, and weak, as a result of both their mixed racial composition and the tropical climate (Flores 1979, chaps. 2, 6). Pedreira's book also reflected the profound influence that *Ariel* had among Latin American intellectuals (Flores 1979, chap. 7).

The ideas of Cuban and Puerto Rican intellectuals were remarkably similar to the racial discourse of Dominican elites. It almost seems as if the three countries—regardless of the fact that their racial composition was different—had the same "national problem." Their elites' preoccupation with their people's mixed racial composition was the result of the dual influence of a racist, Spanish colonial mentality and the racial ideas of nineteenth-century Europe and the United States. The ideas of Herbert Spencer and social Darwinism were particularly influential in Latin America and forced intellectuals to reconsider their societies' racial composition. Since most Latin American—particularly Hispanic Caribbean—societies were highly heterogeneous, most intellectuals selected only those elements of European racial theories that they could fit within their immediate realities (Graham 1990, 2–3). Others, in an effort to avoid obvious contradictions, went to intellectual extremes to bend their national reality to their expectations, even to the point of distorting history.

The dominant ideas behind antihaitianismo ideology fit within this description. The writings of José Ramón López, Federico García Godoy, Américo Lugo, Manuel Arturo Peña Batlle, and Joaquín Balaguer are part of this traditional Latin American preoccupation with race. The influence of *Ariel* is another shared element between Dominican intellectuals and their Hispanic Caribbean counterparts. Actually, if the Haitian element is taken out of the writings of these Dominican intellectuals, they could be referring to any Hispanic Caribbean nation. Therefore, antihaitianismo ideology can be considered as another dimension of the elites' discussion regarding the "national problem" in Hispanic Caribbean societies.

The uniqueness of antihaitianismo as a Hispanic Caribbean dominant ideology lies in the fact that it involves a foreign threat: Haiti. Whereas Cuba and Puerto Rico are islands with significant black and mulatto populations, the Dominican Republic has a large black and mulatto population, plus a mostly black island neighbor. This presumed "Haitian threat" powerfully shaped the racial ideology of Dominican elites. Animosity toward Haiti—and its revolution—was widespread in the Americas (Plummer 1992), particularly in the United States and Cuba, while it reached hysteria levels in Santo Domingo. Thus antihaitianismo ideology simply developed as the local expression of racist ideas prevalent in the Hispanic Caribbean and imported from Europe and the United States.

The use of Haiti also shifted the blame on the "national problem" from the Dominican Republic to its western neighbor. While in Cuba and Puerto Rico the black threat was internal, in the Dominican Republic the black threat was conveniently externalized. That explains how blacks and mulattos "disappeared" in the Dominican Republic (and were replaced by indios), thus eliminating internal threats and contradictions. The enemy, the wave of dangerous "blackness," is foreign; it comes from Haiti. The contradictions of Dominican society, its racial "weaknesses," and even its lack of socioeconomic development stem—according to antihaitianismo ideology—from the Haitian problem. The paradisiacal, "color-blind" nature of Dominican society is in danger of being corrupted and weakened by its troubled neighbor. In the face of such a dangerous alien threat, authoritarian solutions are invoked and justified by Dominican elites (Ariza Hernández 1994; Casals Victoria 1991; Velázquez Mainardi 1991).

It can be concluded that antihaitianismo ideology is not unique. Its fabrication of a mythical "nationhood," its references to "foreign" threats, its discrimination against the alien "other," and its externalization of the threat (represented by the "foreign-origin" racial mixture of the Dominican people) are common elements of dominant racial ideologies. Though antihaitianismo ideology may seem unique due to its use of Haiti as a reference point, Haiti is simply a convenient accessory to disguise the racial and social inequalities of Dominican society, while giving the impression of racial harmony among the Dominican people. The "national problem"— a racially mixed population ruled by a light-skinned elite that wants to maintain its power—remains the same, whether there is a Haiti or not.

What Are the Consequences of Antihaitianismo?

In the Dominican Republic, antihaitianismo ideology has played several roles. First, it has been used as the basis for the discrimination of Haitians, the country's largest ethnic minority. Second, it has been employed as an ideological weapon of control and manipulation of the Dominican people— specifically the dark-skinned lower classes—for it diffuses class tensions and moves the political agenda away from the issue of equitable redistribution of wealth in Dominican society. And third, since its development it has remained a dominant ideology, competing against and subjugating alternative ideas. Antihaitianismo ideology is so ingrained in Dominican culture that antihaitianismo has become the norm, rather than the exception, in Dominican society. In the face of the evidence presented in the previous chapters, what are the immediate and future consequences of antihaitianismo ideology for the Dominican Republic, for Haitian migrants, and for the Haitian-Dominican relationship?

Antihaitianismo and International Relations

The continued predominance of antihaitianismo ideology and the anti-Haitian prejudice that it justifies is bound to affect the Dominican Republic in the international arena in several ways, all of them detrimental to its national interest. A continued record of human rights abuses, in the form of slavelike Haitian labor, could threaten U.S. and European economic aid to the Dominican Republic. Negative publicity surrounding allegations of abuse has caused substantial embarrassment to the Dominican authorities on more than one occasion, forcing the country to expend valuable resources in restoring its public image. Prestigious international organizations, such as the International Labor Organization, Americas Watch, the Anti-Slavery Society, and the AFL-CIO have investigated these allegations. Apparently, the mistreatment to which Haitians have been subjected for decades in the Dominican Republic will no longer be tolerated by the outside world. Besides these international groups, there are now several Dominican and Haitian-Dominican organizations that periodically denounce cases of mistreatment and compile data on human rights abuses which they forward to international agencies.

Though the cases of mistreatment of Haitians and Haitian-Dominicans are not a result of official policies, but of individual actions, many of these cases involve government officials (particularly the military), and typically they act with impunity. Certainly, this is an issue in which the Dominican government is vulnerable to economic sanctions from its main trading partners. As such, the Dominican government should take forceful action to prevent human rights abuses against Haitian immigrants and to sanction government officials who persist in these practices.

Haitian migrants in the Dominican Republic will keep on being exploited as long as antihaitianismo ideology prevails in Dominican culture. Antihaitianismo not only provides the necessary justification for the exploitation of Haitian labor but also has the intended effect of dehumanizing Haitians. A similar fate is suffered by arrayanos, who, even though they are Dominican citizens by birth, are treated, for all practical purposes, as Haitians.

Haitians are the traditional scapegoats of Dominican society. They are periodically blamed for some of the Dominican Republic's internal problems, such as AIDS, unemployment, and the scarcity of basic foodstuffs. These political ploys serve only to worsen the already poor situation of Haitians in the Dominican Republic and to provide additional fuel for the reproduction of antihaitianismo ideology.

Antihaitianismo has also remained a major obstacle for a full normalization and relaxation of Haitian-Dominican relations. Not until Haitian and Dominican leaders learn to set aside their historical differences will the quality of Haitian-Dominican relations improve. Leaders from both Haiti and the Dominican Republic have publicly expressed their desire to enhance the current status of the Haitian-Dominican relationship. However, their actions belie their words. Such was the recent case of Presidents Aristide and Balaguer. Aristide, in an effort to improve his government's popularity, tried to arouse nationalist feelings among the Haitian people by denouncing antihaitianismo and human rights abuses in the Dominican Republic at the United Nations. Balaguer, in retaliation, began the massive repatriation of illegal Haitians living in the Dominican Republic. Actions like these tend only to exacerbate the already tense nature of the relationship and provide little fertile ground for a new dialogue.

The elections of René Préval in Haiti and Leonel Fernández in the Dominican Republic, representatives of a younger generation and a new style of leadership, offer the potential for a closer working relationship. A joint, binational commission was created to draft new agreements, and President Fernández even visited Haiti. However, most of these agreements have been of secondary importance, and the issue of Haitian migration still remains unsolved, as both sides have major differences.

Dominican Democracy and Antihaitianismo

Democracy is a fairly new feature of the Dominican political system. Even though there have been relatively free elections since 1966, it was not until 1978 when, by most accounts, the Dominican Republic became a democratic nation, after the semiauthoritarian Joaquín Balaguer was defeated in his third bid for reelection. Democracy, however, cannot be complete if it protects just one sector of society. For Dominicans to live in a truly democratic system, the rights of Haitian migrants and Haitian-Dominicans must be recognized, not only in theory but also in practice. Unless democratic rights are extended to the country's largest minority, the Dominican Republic will remain a democracy in name only.

The fate of Haitian migrants also affects Dominican democracy in another way. Most calls for a solution to "the Haitian problem" are authoritarian in nature—from forced repatriations to creating a new state in Africa (or somewhere else) to resettle Haiti's excess population. Authoritarian tendencies that already are a feature of the Dominican political system are being reinforced by this aspect of antihaitianismo ideology. Although there are no guarantees that a more liberal handling of the Haitian issue would improve Dominican democracy, the present authoritarian methods clearly are having a deleterious effect on democracy in the Dominican Republic.

As this study has emphasized, antihaitianismo ideology is not only directed toward Haitians. It also affects the Dominican people—particularly dark-skinned, lower-class Dominicans—in several ways. First, antihaitianismo ideology acts as a wedge between two peoples who share a small island and who should learn to peacefully cohabit it. It is ironic to see how common Haitians and Dominicans spite each other while their respective elites exploit their misery. Antihaitianismo ideology is part and parcel of the

Dominican elite's "divide and conquer" policies. They know that ethnically and racially divided lower classes, incapable of forming transnational alliances with their Haitian counterparts, can be exploited and controlled much more easily.

Second, antihaitianismo ideology has prevented Dominicans from recognizing their true racial identity and has perpetuated their racial "confusion" or denial. The heritage of Africa and its contributions to Dominican culture and society have yet to achieve their rightful place among Dominicans. As long as antihaitianismo ideology perpetuates the idea that Dominicans are not "black," the Dominican people will be unable to come to terms with their African heritage. Even though this heritage touches practically all Dominicans, it traditionally has been relegated to a distant place, well behind the fabricated myth of Indian heritage.

Third, antihaitianismo ideology is a method of control in a society still laden with prejudice and authoritarianism. Blacks and dark mulattos are still the target of unofficial discrimination in the Dominican Republic, and every so often black Dominicans are deported to Haiti, regardless of their identity papers proving their Dominican nationality. Moreover, antihaitianismo ideology maintains an archaic—and, it is hoped, now crumbling—socioeconomic structure in which dark-skinned citizens occupy the lower rungs of the social pyramid and are destined to perform mostly manual labor. Even today, dark-skinned Dominicans are widely represented only in sports, entertainment, the military, and politics. On the other hand, dark-skinned Dominicans are woefully underrepresented in business, science, and education. Antihaitianismo ideology helps perpetuate this division and justifies it in the minds of citizens as "the way things are."

Finally, antihaitianismo ideology has been used for settling political scores and discrediting Dominican public figures for decades. Black populist leaders and those who have defended the rights of Haitian migrants have been labeled un-Dominican, and their nationalism has been questioned. The case of President Ulises Heureaux is one example, and so far the most extreme case has been that of black politician José Francisco Peña Gómez. The 1994 and 1996 electoral campaigns were characterized by the use of anti-Haitian "negative advertizing" against Peña Gómez. Regardless of the mudslinging campaign against Peña Gómez, he was a popular politician among Dominicans of all classes and colors, and he obtained well over a million votes in both the 1994 and 1996 elections. Yet in spite of the fact that Peña

Gómez was a capable, well-prepared, and popular candidate, the feelings of enmity that his supposed Haitian ancestry (and other personal characteristics) sparked among his opponents led them to join forces and mount impressive campaigns against him. Probably no other presidential candidate had to face such enormous obstacles as Peña Gómez. In the end, he was defeated in three attempts to become president by forces that relied heavily on the use of antihaitianismo ideology. As long as this mudslinging tactic keeps working so effectively, antihaitianismo will remain an integral part of the Dominican political system and a favorite weapon in Dominican politics.

In summary, antihaitianismo ideology developed from the generally tense and conflictive nature of the Haitian-Dominican relationship and the countries' unequal levels of development, and from the manipulation of anti-Haitian feelings by Dominican elites for the achievement of political ends. Haitian-Dominican relations have often been conflictive, and Dominican elites have deliberately transformed antihaitianismo into a dominant ideology that cuts across Dominican society, to the point of distorting Dominican history and popular culture. Surveys and field research have shown that most Dominicans share a number of prejudices and stereotypes about Haitians that are the result of an intense anti-Haitian socialization process.

Though antihaitianismo is a racist ideology, it is simplistic to just say that Dominicans are racist (Dore Cabral 1995). Race is but one of the multifaceted aspects of antihaitianismo ideology; other components are nationalism, culture, and history. Antihaitianismo ideology resembles a prism where different prejudices and myths are combined in such a way that it is sometimes difficult to distinguish between them. That is precisely the intended effect of antihaitianismo: it is a dominant ideology designed to confuse and mislead. As a result, race is confused with nation: Haitians are black; Dominicans are indios. Haitians believe in voodoo; Dominicans are devout Catholics. Haiti's heritage is African; the Dominican Republic's is Hispanic. It is in these deliberate confusions that antihaitianismo ideology thrives, and that is also why it has been so difficult to eradicate it from Dominican culture.

Moreover, antihaitianismo is a convenient ideology, both for the Dominican elites and for the masses. For the conservative Dominican elites, antihaitianismo ideology helps protect their economic interests by providing a cheap and docile labor force, promoting Dominican nationalism and Hispanic values, and serving as a political weapon against liberal opponents. In general, it is a potent "divide and conquer" strategy. For the Dominican people, antihaitianismo ideology provides a feeling of security based on false ideas of racial and cultural superiority. No matter how bad things may look in the Dominican Republic, Haitians are always doing even worse. And no matter how poor or black a Dominican might be, the Dominican can always feel "superior" to any Haitian because he or she is Dominican, Hispanic, and indio. Antihaitianismo ideology provides a people besieged by economic crises and social inequalities with a flattering but distorted mirror.

The implications of antihaitianismo ideology go far beyond the confines of the island of Hispaniola and the Spanish-speaking Caribbean. The Haitian-Dominican case can offer insights into racial and ethnic prejudice in other countries and serve to illustrate how elites manipulate racial and cultural issues to achieve nationalist political goals. First, the Dominican case shows that racism and prejudice can also be widespread in a highly racially mixed society, where racial gradations are blurred. As social phenomena, racial stereotypes do not necessarily have to agree with our surrounding reality. Thus, it should come as no surprise that in a mulatto country the beauty standard (and the color of power) is white. Second, the Dominican case also shows that the "other" does not have to belong to a different ethnic group; "otherness" can exist within the dominant group. Contrary to cases where the "other" was easily discernible (for example, blacks under South Africa's apartheid system), in the Dominican Republic the "other" is represented by references to blackness in what is an intrinsically Afro-Caribbean nation. Accordingly, the "other" can be a Haitian (who belongs to a different ethnic group), as well as a black Dominican (who belongs to the dominant group but is alienated due to his or her blackness). The rabid prejudice of antihaitianismo ideology owes more to similarities than to differences as it struggles to find—and if not there, to create—differences between the two peoples. Finally, the Dominican case calls for a revision of existing theories of racial and ethnic conflict. Racial conflict—whenever it is politically expedient—can coexist with appeals to myths of racial equality and harmony. Balaguer himself, one of the Dominican Republic's main racial ideologues, has publicly declared that the only prejudice that has ever existed in the country is of a religious nature (1947, 119).

This book attempts to contribute to a better understanding of the way in which "symbolic racism" works in dominant ideologies. In the Dominican Republic, where everyday realities do not always correspond to racial and ethnic attitudes, antihaitianismo ideology is more myth than reality, more talk than substance. Few Dominicans are actually directly threatened by the "Haitian problem," yet most of them seem to hate and/or fear Haitians. A similar case could be argued for other Latin American and postcolonial countries, where the ruling elites have played on racial, ethnic, and cultural cleavages for their own political and economic gains.

Finally, antihaitianismo ideology must be viewed within the context of other racial ideologies in the Hispanic Caribbean. Antihaitianismo ideology, except for its references to Haiti, is not a unique phenomenon. The racial ideologies of Cuban and Puerto Rican intellectuals have been strikingly similar to those of their Dominican counterparts. Since colonial times, class and race have been intrinsically linked in the Hispanic Caribbean, and its elites have created Hispanophile ideologies to maintain their privileged status quo. Racism and prejudice, though not apparent to the casual observer (as a result of widespread miscegenation), underlie the social structure of these nations.

Even today, more than a century after the abolition of slavery in the region, Cuba, Puerto Rico, and the Dominican Republic are ruled by white or light-skinned elites. And as long as ideologies like antihaitianismo remain hegemonic, little meaningful change can be expected. José Francisco Peña Gómez put it bluntly, after being defeated in the second round of the 1996 Dominican elections, in his third unsuccessful attempt to win the presidency: "The Dominican Republic is still not ready for a black president."[2]

APPENDIX A

Dominican Identification Cards

DOMINICANA
NACIONALIDAD

ARROYO DE LECHE PUERTO
LUGAR DE NACIMIENTO

1----5---1965
FECHA DE NACIMIENTO

CASADA   SI   SI
ESTADO CIVIL   ¿ LEE ?   ¿ ESCRIBE ?

ESTUDIANTE
OCUPACION

SANTIAGO, R, D,
DOMICILIO (CIUDAD O PUEBLO)

RESIDENCIA (CALLE Y CASA NO.)

BARRIO, SECTOR O CUARTEL

5   6 PARAJE Y SECCION RURAL **115**
PIES   PULGADAS   ESTATURA   PESO   LIBRAS
COLOR NATURAL DE LA PIEL   **INDIO**

EL PELO **NEGRO** LOS OJOS **NEGROS**

NINGUNAS
MARCAS O SEÑAS VISIBLES DE IDENTIFICACION

TIPO DE SANGRE   ¿ ALERGICO A LA PENICILINA ?

A.1.   Old (pre-1994) Dominican identification card. Note the use of the term *indio* in the skin color category. Author's collection.

A.2.   New Dominican identification card. Notice under the "color" category the use of the letter *I*, which stands for *indio*. Author's collection.

APPENDIX B

Anti-Haitian Political Cartoons from the Dominican Press

B.1.   A poor Haitian migrant tries to enter the Dominican Republic, but he is stopped by a big white hand. By permission of *El Nacional* newspaper, Santo Domingo, Dominican Republic.

B.2.   The Dominican Republic tries to run away from Haiti. The former is drawn with white feet, while the latter has black feet. By permission of *El Nacional* newspaper, Santo Domingo, Dominican Republic.

B.3.   A huge black hand (Haiti) threatens to engulf the Dominican Republic. A white Dominican waves a stop sign. By permission of *El Nacional* newspaper, Santo Domingo, Dominican Republic.

B.4.   A white Dominican makes fun of the allegations by international human rights organizations that Haitian children work in the Dominican sugar fields. "How awful! There are children working here," he comments, while pointing to an adult Haitian cane-cutter with a pacifier in his mouth. By permission of *El Nacional* newspaper, Santo Domingo, Dominican Republic.

B.5.   A parody of Jean-Bertrand Aristide's speech in which he called
Haiti and the Dominican Republic "two wings of the same bird." The
message is obvious: Haiti is considered a huge burden for the Dominican
Republic. By permission of *El Nacional* newspaper, Santo Domingo, Dominican Republic.

APPENDIX C

Anti–Peña Gómez Political Propaganda

C.1.   Anonymous fax. The upper drawing parodies Peña Gómez's warning that violence would ensue if someone tried to assassinate him. The
lower drawing warns Dominicans about their fate if "the Haitian" won the
elections: the Dominican people (on their knees and gagged) would be
overrun by the Haitian masses. Peña Gómez is shown dancing while his
Haitian supporters celebrate. Courtesy of Ricardo R. Fernández.

PEÑA ODIA LA RE.P. DOMINICANA POR LA MATANZA
DE LOS HAITIANOS Y SU PADRES EN EL 1937
SI PEÑA GANA SUCEDE ESTO

CON EL APOYO DE CLINTON Y LOS PAISES EUROPEOS
PEÑA ES UN PELIGRO, CUIDADO !

PEÑA NO ES PRIETO, ES HAITIANO

C.2.   Anonymous fax. A drawing of Hispaniola full of Haitians. The captions read: "Peña hates the Dominican Republic for the massacre of Haitians and his parents in 1937. If Peña wins, this will happen, with the support of Clinton and the European countries. Peña is dangerous, beware! Peña is not black, he is Haitian." Courtesy of Ricardo R. Fernández.

¿Quién es este hombre?
¿Lo conocemos realmente?

Lo que no sabemos de él:

Nosotros no sabemos todo lo que debíamos saber acerca de Peña Gómez.
Por ejemplo, nosotros no sabemos cómo él reaccionaría frente a una emergencia nacional.
No sabemos qué él haría para crear fuentes de trabajo o ayudar al desarrollo de nuestra economía.
No sabemos si él colocará a sus amigos corruptos nuevamente en las oficinas públicas.
No sabemos cuáles son sus planes para el futuro.
Es justo reconocer, pués, que nosotros no sabemos mucho acerca de ESTE hombre.

LO QUE SÍ SABEMOS DE ÉL:

Lo que nosotros sabemos de Peña Gómez no es nada bueno.
Nosotros sabemos que él pierde fácilmente la paciencia y actúa irracionalmente.
Nosotros sabemos que él amenazó, y es capaz de hacerlo, de prenderle fuego a NUESTRA
REPUBLICA DOMINICANA, por los cuatro costados.
Sabemos que él cree en cosas satánicas, y se identifica.
Sabemos que él ha dicho que abriría nuestras fronteras a los haitianos.
Sabemos que él tiene muchos amigos corruptos en el mundo que han sido condenados o se
encuentran sometidos a escandalosos procesos criminales.

PIÉNSALO!

No podemos arriesgar el futuro
de nuestro país con un hombre como ESTE!

_____ PRSC

C.3.   Negative advertisement during the 1994 campaign. Peña Gómez
was shown as an unstable, dangerous individual. The big captions read:
"Who is this man? Do we really know him? What we do not know about
him [and lists details]. What we do know about him [and lists details].
Think about it! We cannot risk the future of our country on a man like
this!" Under the caption of "What we do know about him" are: "We know
that he believes in Satanic practices" and "We know that he has said that he
would open our borders to Haitians." Author's collection.

NOTES

Introduction: Race and Politics

1. All translations are mine, unless otherwise indicated.

2. The population of Cuba is 51 percent mulatto, 37 percent white, 11 percent black, and 1 percent Chinese; the Dominican Republic is 73 percent mulatto, 16 percent white, and 11 percent black; and Puerto Rico is 55 percent white, 40 percent mulatto, and 5 percent black (Goodwin 1992, 104, 110; Wells 1985, 613). All the percentages are rough estimates. In the case of Puerto Rico, the data are from a 1950 census, the last one to include racial categories.

3. See Graham (1990) for a very interesting discussion of these four cases.

4. Elites are defined in van Dijk's work as "social (minority) groups that have various types of power and control, whether political, economic, social, cultural, or personal" (1987, 367).

5. A batey simply consists of a group of houses surrounded by cane fields.

6. For example, the average exchange rate of the Dominican peso went from RD$3.85 per dollar in 1987 to RD$6.11 per dollar in 1988. The annual inflation rate for 1989 was 45.4 percent (Economist Intelligence Unit 1993).

1. Antihaitianismo: From Colonialism to the Twentieth Century

1. Traditional Dominican historians—in a truly exaggerated fashion—have labeled these forms of slavery "paternal" or "benign" slavery. For a sharp rebuttal, see Inoa 1992. On the development of the French colony of Saint-Domingue in western Hispaniola, Moreau de Saint-Méry ([1796] 1944, 7–27) provides a detailed chronological account of the growth of the Tortuga settlement up to the official Spanish recognition of the French colony in 1777.

2. In French Saint-Domingue, it made more economic sense for masters to work their slaves to death and replace them with new ones than to encourage their reproduction (Ott 1973, 17).

3. Gaspar de Arredondo y Pichardo, an upper-class citizen of the time, referred to Dessalines's troops as "cannibals" (Rodríguez Demorizi 1955a, 137).

4. Voodoo (also spelled *vodou*) is the folk religion of Haiti. Its origins can be traced to the beliefs of West African slaves who were forcibly transported to Saint-Domingue, and who also borrowed religious elements from Catholicism (Desmangles 1992).

5. Moi, moi, je suis blanc de cette terre!

6. Writing in the 1790s, Father Juan Vásquez considered Haitians to be "heretics and cannibals" (Jimenes Grullón 1969, 67).

7. The former slaves of Santo Domingo even called the pro-independence movement the "Revolution of the Spaniards." During the struggle for Dominican independence there were rebellious attempts, in which troops were mobilized but there was no bloodshed, and actual rebellions and mutinies by black Dominican leaders and their troops, who feared the reestablishment of slavery (F. J. Franco 1989, 160–62; 1994).

8. Most of the Trinitarios were eventually executed (e.g., Sánchez, the Puello brothers) or sent into exile. Duarte himself died in exile in Venezuela, poor and forgotten. See Balaguer (1994) for a romantic novel on the life of Juan Pablo Duarte, and R. Martínez (1971) for biographical data on the Trinitarios.

9. It is ironic that Báez himself was the subject of racist remarks made by his political enemies, owing to his humble origins and his dark color.

10. Sánchez's execution presents a poignant example of the racist attitudes of the Spanish colony. After the death squad shot him, his executioner supposedly remarked, "Laugh now, little Negro" (Balcácer 1977, 26).

11. The project made it to the U.S. Senate, where it was defeated by a few votes (Welles 1986, 1:374).

12. For example, Dominican Hispanophile historian Emilio Rodríguez Demorizi defended the "Indian obsession" of the Dominican people by pointing out the fact that Haiti—which according to Rodríguez Demorizi cannot claim any Indian ancestry for its people—also had an indigenista literature (Rodríguez Demorizi 1955a, 49–52).

13. Today, *Enriquillo* is considered the national novel of the Dominican Republic, and it is required reading for all students. For a literary examination of *Enriquillo,* see Sommer 1991.

14. The romanticization of the Indian past and the myth of the *indio* identity are not unique to the Dominican people. Cuba and Puerto Rico have their own Indian national myths (Roberts 1997). Other Latin American countries with a strong African heritage, such as Brazil, have also created similar Indian myths and developed racist ideologies (Skidmore 1993).

15. To this day, the word *mulatto* is rarely used in the Dominican Republic; most people use the term *indio.*

16. Hostos (1839–1903), of Puerto Rican origin, is considered the father of education in the Dominican Republic, as his secular, scientific ideas revolutionized and tried

to displace traditional Catholic education. For his achievements he was revered as "El Maestro" (The Teacher).

17. Heureaux's father was Haitian, while his mother was an immigrant from the Lesser Antilles.

18. *Mañé* is a demeaning term used for Haitians.

19. Quisqueya (supposedly) was an Indian name for the island of Hispaniola.

20. There has been a scholarly debate about the anti-Haitian attitudes of Américo Lugo. While Emilio Rodríguez Demorizi (1955a, 40–44) and Lil Despradel (1974, 102–3) use Lugo's racist, anti-Haitian arguments in a legal case as the basis for their claim, Bernardo Vega (1988, 29–30) contends that, on that occasion, Lugo was simply acting as a defense lawyer, and that these legal arguments did not reflect the feelings of Lugo the intellectual.

2. Antihaitianismo and State Ideology during the Trujillo Era

1. Baud (1993a, 1993b) and Derby (1994) examine in detail the way of life of the fronterizos before the 1937 massacre.

2. Trujillo's troops, for obvious reasons, refrained from killing Haitians who worked in the mostly U.S.-owned sugar plantations. Vega (1988, 385–87) compiled a list of the various figures published on the number of Haitians killed in the 1937 massacre. In a recent publication, he estimates that only 4,000 to 6,000 Haitians were actually killed (1995, chap. 9).

3. Just days after the massacre, Secretary of State of Justice Julio Ortega Frier commented on the desire of the Trujillo administration to rid the Dominican Republic of black Haitians and to promote "white" immigration, particularly from Puerto Rico (Vega 1988, 395–96). The 1937 massacre, it seems, was the first step in this direction.

4. By the late 1930s, most of the intellectuals who still opposed the Trujillo regime had gone into exile or suffered from constant harassment and ostracism. The most notorious case was Américo Lugo, whom Trujillo unsuccessfully tried to co-opt, and who died poor and alone, shunned by the regime.

5. Ironically, even though Trujillo had Haitian ancestry on his mother's side, his disdain for Haitians and his admiration for Spain were well known. He even went to the extreme of using makeup to lighten his skin tone (Crassweller 1966, 95; Diederich and Burt 1986, 12).

6. This book won the 1944 essay prize in a contest held by the Ateneo Dominicano (Dominican Atheneum, a cultural organization), in commemoration of the one hundredth anniversary of Dominican independence.

7. This volume was originally published in French as *La République d'Haïti et la République Dominicaine* (see Price-Mars 1953). The forefather of an entire generation of Haitian scholars, Jean Price-Mars was one of the brightest Haitian intellectuals of his time. He also served in various government positions, including a stint as Haitian ambassador to Ciudad Trujillo in the 1940s.

8. The "goat without horns" is an anthropophagic practice attributed by Rosario

Pérez to Haitian voodoo practitioners. It consists of a presumed voodoo ceremony in which a human baby is sacrificed and then devoured by some of the participants (Rosario Pérez 1957, 98).

3. Antihaitianismo as a Political Tool for Trujillo

1. Trujillo actually loved to be called *jefe* (boss) by his subordinates.

2. For a detailed description of the Dominicanization of the border region, see Machado Báez (1955, chaps. 21–24).

3. Trujillo occasionally allowed the creation of other political parties to give the impression that a multiparty system existed in the Dominican Republic. Some of those parties also nominated Trujillo for the presidency, others presented a fictitious opposition, and others were only allowed to organize during certain periods, and then quickly disbanded.

4. All public employees had to be members of the PD and were forced to contribute 10 percent of their salaries to the party. For the 1942 elections, Trujillo extended suffrage to women, in an effort to include virtually all adult Dominicans in the PD. For all practical purposes, the identification card of the PD was an indispensable document for any adult, along with the national identity card and the compulsory military service card (Inoa 1994, 74).

5. The alcalde pedáneo was a very important figure of the Trujillo regime. Selected from among the most loyal and most influential men of a rural section, the alcalde pedáneo was the representative of the Trujillista state in the countryside. His duties included maintaining peace and order, settling disputes, and, most important, keeping Trujillo informed of everything that was taking place in the Dominican countryside.

6. A cursory examination of the social pages of any Dominican newspaper will attest to this fact. Or see, for example, the magazine *Viú.*

7. For the 1960 census, interviewers were instructed to categorize as white anyone "who was not evidently black" (Moya Pons 1986b, 246).

4. Antihaitianismo Ideology in the Post-Trujillo Period

1. This is a veiled reference to the 1937 massacre, portrayed by Trujillo's propagandists as a sporadic act of retribution against Haitian cattle rustlers.

2. *La isla al revés* caused intense controversies when it was published. For some excellent reviews of *La isla al revés,* see Dore Cabral (1985); Fennema and Loewenthal (1987); and Zaglul (1992).

3. Efforts are now under way to reform the teaching of Dominican history at all levels. In 1998, new, more objective Dominican history textbooks were introduced into the public school curricula.

4. Estella and Alloza were both Spanish immigrants, refugees from the Spanish Civil War (1936–39) who were admitted into the country by dictator Trujillo. The long-

lasting impact of that immigration on Dominican society is examined by Vega (1991, 275–83).

5. The closest translation of the term *indio* (Indian) would be "Indianlike," as it refers to skin color (mulatto) and racial features (hair, lips, nose, etc.), rather than to the ethnic group that originally inhabited the island.

6. Richard Reeves describes political cartoons as "simply the shortest distance between one point and one citizen." See, for example, Nancy King's *A Cartoon History of United States Foreign Policy from 1945 to the Present* (New York: Pharos Books, 1991).

7. It must be kept in mind that for many uneducated individuals a million is not a precise number but a way of indicating a very large quantity. The figure of "a million" Haitians living in the Dominican Republic has also been promoted in the media in order to create the impression of an uncontrollable flood of Haitians taking over the country (Puig 1992, 62–63).

8. The twenty-seventh of February is Dominican Independence Day. It is a very symbolic day, with all the fanfare of an American fourth of July, but charged with nationalist speeches focusing on the liberation struggle against the Haitian occupiers.

9. The respondent was obviously referring to the 1937 massacre, when Trujillo ordered the assassination of thousands of Haitians living in the Dominican Republic.

10. The term *arrayano* (or *rayano*) is used in the Dominican Republic to designate a person born in the Dominican Republic but of Haitian origin. That is, at least one parent (usually the mother), or even a grandparent, is Haitian. The word *arrayano* comes from the Spanish *raya* (line), a reference to the borderline. Dore Cabral (1987) uses the more formal term *rayano,* which has been popularly transformed into *arrayano.* Arrayanos are a living borderline; half-Haitian, half-Dominican. For practical purposes, however, they are neither one nor the other. Most Dominicans consider them to be Haitians (even though they were born in the Dominican Republic and most of them do not know Haiti), while Haitians do not think of them as their fellow countrymen since, again, most of them do not know Haiti and/or they cannot speak fluent Creole.

11. Here the respondent was reproducing a popular myth widely employed in grade school to emphasize the atrocities committed during the Haitian occupation of the Dominican Republic. Although barbaric acts were certainly committed by the Haitian armies, only the worst aspects of the Haitian occupation seem to be emphasized in school. As a result, this image of the barbaric Haitian invader has become an integral part of the popular culture and is quickly recalled by lower-class Dominicans whenever they talk about the Haitian occupation of the Dominican Republic.

12. In a survey in which respondents were asked if they would marry a Haitian individual (or agree to a close relative marrying a Haitian individual), the strongest opposition came from lower-class Dominicans (Dore Cabral 1995).

13. Murphy (1991, 139–41), in his study of the Dominican sugar industry, found that the poorest Dominican workers (i.e., those who worked alongside Haitians) were less prejudiced than workers who occupied semispecialized or managerial positions. That is, those Dominican workers who were in direct contact with Haitians—thus getting to know them better—feared and hated them less. National surveys, on the

other hand, have found the greatest degree of prejudice among lower-class Dominicans (Dore Cabral 1995).

5. Balaguer and the Cohabitation of Antihaitianismo with Democracy

1. Whether Bosch had any knowledge of the activities of Haitian exiles on Dominican territory has been fiercely debated. Bosch (1965) himself has denied it. Historian Roberto Cassá, on the other hand, finds it extremely doubtful (not to say distressing) for a Dominican president to be completely unaware of such activities taking place within the national territory (1991, 96–97). Less clear is the role played by the Kennedy administration and the CIA, which wanted to get rid of Duvalier. According to journalist Víctor Grimaldi (1985)—an apologist of Bosch—it was the CIA and the Kennedy administration that prompted Bosch's overthrown, so as to cover up their role in this affair. More recently, Vega (1993a, iv–v) asserts that Bosch—at least initially—actively supported the Haitian exile groups.

2. *Amba fil,* a Haitian Creole term, literally means "under the wire," a reference to the surreptitious way in which Haitian migrant workers illegally cross the border.

3. *Lavalas* means "torrential rain" or "deluge," an analogy to the movement's popular strength and its ability (just like rain) to clean. In this case, it sought to "clean" the Haitian political system of Duvalierist elements and practices.

4. It took the Junta Central Electoral, the Dominican Republic's electoral board, more than two months to declare a winner. On 2 August 1994, two weeks before the new president was to be sworn in, Balaguer was formally declared winner of the 1994 national elections.

5. In contrast, the three other main presidential candidates, Joaquín Balaguer, Juan Bosch, and Jacobo Majluta, were white.

6. In voodoo, it is believed that a spirit (*luá*) can "mount" a believer, just as a horseman mounts his horse. While "mounted," the person assumes the personality of the luá until the latter decides to leave the body. For a study of Afro-Caribbean religious beliefs in the Dominican Republic, see Deive (1992).

7. The use of the word *perejil* (a form of parsley) dates back to the 1937 massacre. Supposedly, dark-skinned persons were required to say *perejil* in order for the military to establish their nationality. If the person had difficulty pronouncing *perejil* with a clear Spanish accent, he or she was considered a Haitian and killed on the spot.

8. The PRD alleged that as many as 200,000 of their sympathizers were purposely excluded from the voting lists and were thus unable to cast their ballots.

9. If no candidate obtained more than 50 percent of the votes in the first round, the two candidates with the most votes would then participate in a run-off election to be held forty-five days later (República Dominicana 1994).

10. Interestingly enough, the ad used the word *moreno* for black, instead of the more racially conflictive (and Haitian-related) *negro.*

11. The Dominican Congress is composed of a Senate and a Cámara de Diputados (House of Deputies). In the 1994 elections, the PLD obtained 1 senator (out of 30) and

13 deputies (out of 120); the PRD, 15 senators and 57 deputies; and the PRSC, 14 senators and 50 deputies.

12. Nevertheless, a vote for Peña Gómez was not an indicator of lack of anti-Haitian prejudices. There is no reason to believe that anti-Haitian prejudices among PRD sympathizers are any less common than among the general public. It just seems that they did not believe the propaganda of Peña Gómez's opponents.

13. Speaking of images, the main presidential candidates hired consultants to fabricate an attractive image for the 1994 campaign. Balaguer's campaign picture was a hand-drawn portrait, in which he looked considerably younger and vigorous (with rosy cheeks!). Peña Gómez's campaign picture was a retouched photo, in which his Negroid features were noticeably softened, so as to give him a more Caucasian look (see Leonor 1994).

14. As part of that ultranationalist campaign, Balaguer also issued a decree requiring all radio stations to play the Dominican national anthem at noon.

Conclusion: The Political Manipulation of Race

1. See the survey published by *Rumbo* (a Dominican news magazine) on racial attitudes among the Dominican population (Dore Cabral 1995).

2. The Dominican Republic has only had three black presidents, all of them nineteenth-century military strongmen: Gregorio Luperón, Gaspar Polanco, and Ulises Heureaux. Cuba and Puerto Rico have never had a black head of state.

REFERENCES

Abbott, Elizabeth. 1991. *Haiti: The Duvaliers and Their Legacy.* New York: Touchstone.

Abercrombie, Nicholas, Stephen Hill, and Bryan S. Turner. 1980. *The Dominant Ideology Thesis.* London: George Allen and Unwin.

Álvarez Vega, Bienvenido. 1985. "Problemas de candidatos." *El Nacional,* 8 November, 35.

Anderson, Benedict. 1991. *Imagined Communities: Reflections on the Origin and Spread of Nationalism.* London: Verso.

Ariza Hernández, Marino. 1994. "Consideraciones: Gran preocupación de la Unión Nacionalista." *Listín Diario,* 23 April, 7.

Austerlitz, Paul. 1997. *Merengue: Dominican Music and Dominican Identity.* Philadelphia: Temple University Press.

Avelino, Francisco Antonio. 1966. *Las ideas políticas en Santo Domingo.* Santo Domingo: Editorial Arte y Cine.

Balaguer, Joaquín. 1947. *La realidad dominicana: Semblanza de un país y de un régimen.* Buenos Aires: Imprenta Ferrari Hermanos.

———. 1962. *El centinela de la frontera: Vida y hazañas de Antonio Duvergé.* Buenos Aires: Artes Gráficas.

———. 1984. *La isla al revés: Haití y el destino dominicano.* Santo Domingo: Librería Dominicana.

———. 1994. *El Cristo de la libertad: Vida de Juan Pablo Duarte.* Santo Domingo: Editora Corripio.

Balcácer, Juan Daniel. 1977. "Los dominicanos y la discriminación racial." *¡Ahora!* 695:25–27.

Balibar, Etienne, and Immanuel Wallerstein. 1991. *Race, Nation, Class: Ambiguous Identities.* London: Verso.

[Barskett, James, Sir?]. [1818] 1971. *History of the Island of St. Domingo, from Its First Discovery by Columbus to the Present Period.* Reprint. Westport, Conn.: Negro Universities Press.

Baud, Michiel. 1993a. "Una frontera para cruzar: La sociedad rural a través de la frontera domínico-haitiana (1870–1930)." *Estudios Sociales* 26(94):5–28.

———. 1993b. "Una frontera-refugio: Dominicanos y haitianos contra el Estado (1870–1930)." *Estudios Sociales* 26(92):39–64.

———. 1996. "'Constitutionally White': The Forging of a National Identity in the Dominican Republic." In *Ethnicity in the Caribbean: Essays in Honor of Harry Hoetink*, ed. Gert Oostindie. London: Macmillan Caribbean.

Baur, John Edward. 1947. "Mulatto Machiavelli, Jean Pierre Boyer, and the Haiti of His Day." *Journal of Negro History* 32(3):307–53.

Bellegarde, Dantès. 1953. *Histoire du peuple haïtien (1492–1952).* Port-au-Prince: Collection du Tricinquantenaire de l'Indépendance d'Haïti.

Betances, Agapito B. 1985. "El racismo integrante del antihaitianismo haitiano." *Estudios Sociales* 18(59):61–76.

Betances, Emilio. 1995. *State and Society in the Dominican Republic.* Boulder, Colo.: Westview Press.

Black, Jan Knippers. 1986. *The Dominican Republic: Politics and Development in an Unsovereign State.* Boston: Allen and Unwin.

Bluhm, William T. 1974. *Ideologies and Attitudes: Modern Political Culture.* Englewood Cliffs, N.J.: Prentice-Hall.

Bonó, Pedro Francisco. 1980. *Papeles de Pedro Francisco Bonó: Para la historia de las ideas políticas en Santo Domingo.* 2nd ed. Ed. Emilio Rodríguez Demorizi. Barcelona, Spain: Gráficas M. Pareja.

Bosch, Juan. 1965. *The Unfinished Experiment: Democracy in the Dominican Republic.* New York: Praeger.

Box, Louk, and Barbara de la Rive Box-Lasocki. 1989. "¿Sociedad fronteriza o frontera social? Transformaciones sociales en la zona fronteriza de la República Dominicana (1907–1984)." *Boletín de Estudios Latinoamericanos y del Caribe* 46:49–69.

Brea, Ramonina. 1985. "La cultura nacional: Encuentros y desencuentros." *Ciencia y Sociedad* 10(1):45–53.

Calder, Bruce J. 1984. *The Impact of Intervention: The Dominican Republic during the U.S. Occupation of 1916–1924.* Austin, Tex.: University of Texas Press.

Caroit, Jean-Michel. 1992. "La responsabilidad de los medios de comunicación." In *Ayiti-República Dominicana: En el umbral de los años 90,* ed. CIPROS. Santo Domingo: CIPROS.

Carvajal, Carmen. 1993. "Vicecanciller Herrera Cabral descarta integración RD-Haití." *Listín Diario,* 25 January, 16.

Casado, Fernando. 1998. "República Dominicana: Historia y Cultura: Música, ritmos y bailes." Secretaría de Estado de Turismo. Electronic document. http://www.dominicana.com.do/cultura/ritmo.html

Casals Victoria, Pedro Manuel. 1991. "Aristide: Amenaza y peligro." *El Nacional,* 27 September.

Cassá, Roberto. 1975. "El racismo en la ideología de la clase dominante dominicana." *Ciencia* 3(1):59–85.

———. 1982. "Las manifestaciones ideológicas de la dictadura trujillista." *Cuadernos de Post-grado UASD* 2:57–96.

———. 1991. *Los doce años: Contrarrevolución y desarrollismo.* 2nd ed. Santo Domingo: Editora Búho.

———. 1992. *Historia social y económica de la República Dominicana.* 11th ed. 2 vols. Santo Domingo: Alfa y Omega.

Castillo, José del. 1978. *La inmigración de braceros azucareros en la República Dominicana, 1900–1930.* Santo Domingo: Cuadernos del CENDIA/UASD.

———. 1982. "Azúcar y braceros: Historia de un problema." *Eme-Eme Estudios Dominicanos* 10(58):3–19.

Castor, Suzy. 1987. *Migraciones y relaciones internacionales: El caso haitiano-dominicano.* Santo Domingo: UASD.

Charles, Carolle. 1992. "La raza: Una categoría significativa en el proceso de inserción de los trabajadores haitianos en República Dominicana." In *La cuestión haitiana en Santo Domingo,* ed. Wilfredo Lozano. Santo Domingo: FLACSO.

Chehabi, H. E., and Juan J. Linz. 1998. *Sultanistic Regimes.* Baltimore, Md.: Johns Hopkins University Press.

Christenson, Reo M., Alan S. Engel, Dan N. Jacobs, Mostafa Rejai, and Herbert Waltzer. 1981. *Ideologies and Modern Politics.* 3rd ed. New York: Harper and Row.

CIPROS. 1992. *Ayiti-República Dominicana: En el umbral de los años 90.* Santo Domingo: CIPROS.

"Con hondo sentido sociológico y dominicanista se enfoca el problema de las escuelas fronterizas." 1938. *Boletín del Partido Dominicano,* 10 March, 3, 7.

Congreso Nacional de la República Dominicana. 1943. "Ley 391 que establece penas correccionales para las personas que practiquen los espectáculos de 'voudou' o 'luá.'" *Gaceta Oficial* 5976:14–15.

———. 1951. "Ley Orgánica de Educación, No. 2909." *Gaceta Oficial* 7302:3–32.

Coradín, Víctor M. 1940. *Luá Candelo.* La Vega: Imprenta La Palabra.

Cordero Michel, José R. 1975. *Análisis de la Era de Trujillo (Informe sobre la República Dominicana, 1959).* Santo Domingo: UASD.

Crassweller, Robert D. 1966. *Trujillo: The Life and Times of a Caribbean Dictator.* New York: Macmillan.

Cuello, José Israel. 1985. *Documentos del conflicto domínico-haitiano de 1937.* Santo Domingo: Taller.

———. 1991. "¡Ay, Titid!, ¡Nunca, jamás!" *El Siglo,* 9 October, 7.

D'Agostino, Thomas J. 1992. "The Evolution of an Emerging Political Party System: A Study of Party Politics in the Dominican Republic, 1961–1990." Ph.D. diss. Syracuse University.

Dawson, Richard E., and Kenneth Prewitt. 1969. *Political Socialization.* Boston: Little, Brown.

Deive, Carlos Esteban. 1976. "El prejuicio racial en el folklore dominicano." *Boletín del Museo del Hombre Dominicano* 4(8):75–96.

———. 1980. *La esclavitud del negro en Santo Domingo (1492–1844)*. 2 vols. Santo Domingo: Museo del Hombre Dominicano.

———. 1992. *Vodú y magia en Santo Domingo*. 3rd ed. Santo Domingo: Fundación Cultural Dominicana.

Delince, Kern. 1993. *Les forces politiques en Haïti: Manuel d'histoire contemporaine*. Paris: Éditions Karthala.

Derby, Lauren. 1994. "Haitians, Magic, and Money: *Raza* and Society in the Haitian-Dominican Borderlands, 1900 to 1937." *Comparative Studies in Society and History* 36(3):488–526.

Derby, Robin L. H., and Richard Turits. 1993. "Historias de terror y los terrores de la historia: La masacre haitiana de 1937 en la República Dominicana." *Estudios Sociales* 26(92):65–76.

Desmangles, Leslie G. 1992. *The Faces of the Gods: Vodou and Roman Catholicism in Haiti*. Chapel Hill, N.C.: University of North Carolina Press.

Despradel, Alberto. 1975. "El personaje haitiano en la época de Trujillo." *¡Ahora!* 619:52–54, 56.

———. 1976. "Incidencia racial en la separación dominicana de 1844." *¡Ahora!* 670:34–38.

Despradel, Lil. 1974. "Las etapas del antihaitianismo en la República Dominicana: El papel de los historiadores." In *Política y sociología en Haití y la República Dominicana*, ed. Gérard Pierre-Charles. Mexico: UNAM.

Di Pietro, Giovanni. 1996. *Las mejores novelas dominicanas y bibliografía de la novela dominicana*. San Juan: Isla Negra.

Diederich, Bernard, and Al Burt. 1986. *Papa Doc y los Tontons Macoutes: La verdad sobre Haití*. Santo Domingo: Fundación Cultural Dominicana.

Dore Cabral, Carlos. 1985. "La inmigración haitiana y el componente racista de la cultura dominicana (Apuntes para una crítica a "La isla al revés")." *Ciencia y Sociedad* 10(1):61–69.

———. 1987. "Los dominicanos de origen haitiano y la segregación social en la República Dominicana." *Estudios Sociales* 20(68):57–80.

———. 1995. "La población dominicana, más antihaitiana que racista." *Rumbo* 69:8–10, 12.

Duarte, Isis, Ramonina Brea, Ramón Tejada Holguín, and Clara Báez. 1995. *La cultura política de los dominicanos: Entre el autoritarismo y la democracia*. Santiago: PUCMM.

Economist Intelligence Unit, The. 1993. *EIU Country Profile 1992/93: Dominican Republic, Haiti, Puerto Rico*. London: The Economist.

Equipo Onè-Respe. 1995. *Informe de investigación acerca del prejuicio antihaitiano en la ciudad de Santiago, de la República Dominicana: Un aporte a la comprensión y al acercamiento de dos pueblos*. Santo Domingo: Editora Búho.

Esman, Milton J. 1973. "The Management of Communal Conflict." *Public Policy* 21(1):49–78.

Estella, José Ramón, and José Alloza. [1944] 1986. *Historia gráfica de la República Dominicana*. Reprint. Ed. José Israel Cuello H. Santo Domingo: Taller.

Farmer, Paul. 1994. *The Uses of Haiti.* Monroe, Maine: Common Courage Press.

Fennema, Meindert, and Troetje Loewenthal. 1987. *Construcción de raza y nación en República Dominicana.* Santo Domingo: UASD.

Ferguson, James. 1992. *The Dominican Republic: Beyond the Lighthouse.* London: Latin America Bureau.

Fignolé, Daniel. 1948. *Notre Neybe ou Leur Bahoruco?.* Port-au-Prince: Imprimerie V. Valcin.

Flores, Juan. 1979. *Insularismo e ideología burguesa (Nueva lectura de A. S. Pedreira).* Río Piedras, P.R.: Ediciones Huracán.

Fox, Richard G., ed. 1990. *Nationalist Ideologies and the Production of National Cultures.* Washington, D.C.: American Anthropological Association.

Franco, Franklin J. 1973. "Antihaitianismo e ideología del Trujillato." In *Problemas domínico-haitianos y del Caribe,* ed. Gérard Pierre-Charles. Mexico: UNAM.

———. 1979. *Santo Domingo: Cultura, política e ideología.* Santo Domingo: Editora Nacional.

———. 1981. *Historia de las ideas políticas en la República Dominicana (Contribución a su estudio).* Santo Domingo: Editora Nacional.

———. 1989. *Los negros, los mulatos y la nación dominicana.* 8th ed. Santo Domingo: Editora Nacional.

Franco, Pericles A. 1940. "Perspectiva presente y futura de la Escuela Dominicana a favor de la renovación pedagógica auspiciada por el Gobierno bajo la inspiración del Generalísimo Trujillo." *Boletín del Partido Dominicano* 65:1–8.

French, Howard W. 1994a. "A Dominican's 2 Burdens: Haiti and Balaguer." *New York Times,* 14 April.

———. 1994b. "Embargo Creates 'Oil Boom' Near Haitian Border." *New York Times,* 13 March.

"Fusión, tema de campaña." 1994. *Rumbo* 1(16):34.

Galván, Manuel de Jesús. 1882. *Enriquillo: Leyenda histórica dominicana (1503–1533).* Santo Domingo: Imprenta de García Hermanos.

García, José Gabriel. [1878] 1968. *Compendio de la historia de Santo Domingo.* 4th ed. 4 vols. Santo Domingo: Publicaciones ¡Ahora!.

Gimbernard, Jacinto. 1974. *Historia de Santo Domingo.* 5th ed. Santo Domingo: Editora Cultural Dominicana.

Ginebra, Augusto. 1940. *Principales deberes de un buen alcalde pedáneo en la Era de Trujillo.* Puerto Plata: n.p.

González, Raymundo. 1987. "Notas sobre el pensamiento socio-político dominicano." *Estudios Sociales* 20(67):1–22.

———. 1994. "Peña Batlle y su concepto histórico de la nación dominicana." *Ecos* 2(3):11–52.

González Canalda, María Filomena, and Rubén Silié. 1985. "La nación dominicana en la enseñanza de la historia a nivel primario." *Eme-Eme Estudios Dominicanos* 14(79): 15–29.

González Herrera, Julio. 1943. *Trementina, clerén y bongó.* Ciudad Trujillo: Editorial Pol Hermanos.

Goodwin, Jr., Paul B., ed. 1998. *Global Studies: Latin America.* 8th ed. Guilford, Conn.: Dushkin Publishing Group.

Graham, Richard, ed. 1990. *The Idea of Race in Latin America, 1870–1940.* Austin, Tex.: University of Texas Press.

Grasmuck, Sherri. 1983. "International Stair-Step Migration: Dominican Labor in the United States and Haitian Labor in the Dominican Republic." In *Research in the Sociology of Work,* vol. 2, *Peripheral Workers,* ed. Ida Harper Simpson and Richard L. Simpson. Greenwich, Conn.: Jai Press.

Grimaldi, Víctor. 1985. *El misterio del golpe de 1963.* Santo Domingo: Amigo del Hogar.

Hartlyn, Jonathan. 1998a. *The Struggle for Democratic Politics in the Dominican Republic.* Chapel Hill, N.C.: University of North Carolina Press.

———. 1998b. "The Trujillo Regime in the Dominican Republic." In *Sultanistic Regimes,* ed. H. E. Chehabi and Juan J. Linz. Baltimore, Md.: Johns Hopkins University Press.

Heinl, Robert D., and Nancy G. Heinl. 1978. *Written in Blood: The Story of the Haitian People, 1492–1971.* Boston: Houghton Mifflin.

Helg, Aline. 1990. "Race in Argentina and Cuba, 1880–1930: Theory, Policies, and Popular Reaction." In *The Idea of Race in Latin America, 1870–1940,* ed. Richard Graham. Austin, Tex.: University of Texas Press.

Heneken, Teodoro Stanley [Britannicus, pseud.]. [1852] 1959. "La República Dominicana y el Emperador Sou:louque." In *Documentos para la historia de la República Dominicana,* vol. 3, ed. Emilio Rodríguez Demorizi. Ciudad Trujillo: Impresora Dominicana.

Hernández Franco, Tomás. 1943. "Síntesis, magnitud y solución de un problema." *Cuadernos Dominicanos de Cultura* 1:77–89.

Herraiz, Ismael. 1957. *Trujillo dentro de la historia.* Madrid: Ediciones Acies.

Hobsbawn, Eric. 1994. "The Nation as Invented Tradition." In *Nationalism,* ed. John Hutchinson and Anthony D. Smith. Oxford: Oxford University Press.

Hoetink, Harry. 1971. *Caribbean Race Relations: A Study of Two Variants.* London: Oxford University Press.

———. 1982. *The Dominican People, 1850–1900: Notes for a Historical Sociology.* Trans. Stephen K. Ault. Baltimore, Md.: Johns Hopkins University Press.

———. 1994. *Santo Domingo y el Caribe: Ensayos sobre historia y sociedad.* Santo Domingo: Fundación Cultural Dominicana.

Horowitz, Donald L. 1985. *Ethnic Groups in Conflict.* Berkeley, Calif.: University of California Press.

Hutchinson, John, and Anthony D. Smith, eds. 1996. *Ethnicity.* Oxford: Oxford University Press.

Inoa, Orlando. 1992. "El mito de la esclavitud patriarcal en Santo Domingo." *El Siglo,* 16 November, 7.

———. 1993. "Huida de negros dominicanos durante la Matanza de 1937." *El Siglo,* 18 May, 7.

———. 1994. *Estado y campesinos al inicio de la Era de Trujillo.* Santo Domingo: Librería La Trinitaria.

Jimenes Grullón, Juan Isidro. 1969. "Génesis, desarrollo y finalidad del anti-haitianismo en nuestro país." *¡Ahora!* 270:66–69.

Jiménez, Manuel. 1996. "Rechazo a Peña une Bosch y JB." *Hoy,* 3 June, 1, 7.

Jiménez, Ramón Darío. 1993. *La venganza de Peña Gómez: El regreso de Dessalines.* San Juan: Editora El Dominicano.

Jiménez, Ramón Emilio. 1953. *Trujillo, renovador de una nacionalidad.* Ciudad Trujillo: Secretaría de Estado de Educación y Bellas Artes.

Johnson-Cartee, Karen S., and Gary A. Copeland. 1991. *Negative Political Advertising: Coming of Age.* Hillsdale, N.J.: Lawrence Erlbaum Associates.

Jorge, Bernarda. 1982. "Bases ideológicas de la práctica musical durante la Era de Trujillo." *Eme-Eme Estudios Dominicanos* 10(59):65–99.

Kinder, Donald R., and David O. Sears. 1981. "Prejudice and Politics: Symbolic Racism versus Racial Threats to the Good Life." *Journal of Personality and Social Psychology* 40(3):414–31.

Knight, Franklin W. 1990. *The Caribbean: The Genesis of a Fragmented Nationalism.* 2nd ed. New York: Oxford University Press.

Korngold, Ralph. 1965. *Citizen Toussaint.* New York: Hill and Wang.

Krueger, Richard A. 1988. *Focus Groups: A Practical Guide for Applied Research.* Newbury Park, Calif.: Sage Publications.

Kryzanek, Michael J. 1978. "Diversion, Subversion and Repression: The Strategies of Anti-Opposition Politics in Balaguer's Dominican Republic." *Caribbean Studies* 17(1–2):83–103.

Landolfi, Ciriaco. 1981. *Evolución cultural dominicana, 1844–1899.* Santo Domingo: UASD.

Latorre, Eduardo. 1979. *Política dominicana contemporánea.* Santo Domingo: INTEC.

Lee, Kwan Youl. 1991. "Issues, Images, Symbols, and Negative Attacks in Presidential Campaign TV Commercials from 1952 to 1988." Ph.D. diss. University of Connecticut.

Lemonnier-Delafosse, Jean Baptiste. [1846] 1946. *Segunda campaña de Santo Domingo: Guerra domínico-francesa de 1808.* Trans. Lic. C. Armando Rodríguez. Santiago: Editorial El Diario.

Leonor, Patricia. 1994. "El rostro electoral de los candidatos." *El Siglo,* 30 April, 1-C.

Linz, Juan J. 1970. "An Authoritarian Regime: Spain." In *Mass Politics: Studies in Political Sociology,* ed. Erik Allardt and Stein Rokkan. New York: Free Press.

Logroño, Arturo. 1912. *Compendio didáctico de historia patria.* Santo Domingo: Impresora la Cuna de América.

López, José Ramón. [1896] 1955. "La alimentación y las razas." *Revista Dominicana de Cultura* 1(1):73–112.

López de Santa Anna, Antonio. 1958. *Misión fronteriza.* Dajabón: n.p.

Lozano, Wilfredo, and Franc Báez Evertsz. 1992. *Migración internacional y economía cafetalera: Estudio sobre la migración estacional de trabajadores haitianos a la cosecha cafetalera en la República Dominicana.* 2nd ed. Santo Domingo: CEPAE.

Lugo, Américo. [1916] 1949. "El Estado dominicano ante el derecho público." In *Antología.* Ciudad Trujillo: Librería Dominicana.

Lundahl, Mats. 1979. *Peasants and Poverty: A Study of Haiti.* New York: St. Martin's Press.

Machado Báez, Manuel A. 1955. *La dominicanización fronteriza.* Ciudad Trujillo: Impresora Dominicana.

Mackenzie, Charles. [1830] 1971. *Notes on Haiti, Made during a Residence in that Republic.* 2 vols. Reprint. London: Frank Cass.

Madiou, Thomas. [1847] 1981. *Histoire d'Haïti.* 8 vols. Reprint. Port-au-Prince: Éditions Henri Deschamps.

Marrero Aristy, Ramón. 1939. *Over.* Ciudad Trujillo: Imprenta La Opinión.

Martínez, Rufino. 1971. *Diccionario biográfico-histórico dominicano, 1821–1930.* Santo Domingo: UASD.

Martínez, Samuel. 1995. *Peripheral Migrants: Haitians and Dominican Republic Sugar Plantations.* Knoxville, Tenn.: University of Tennessee Press.

———. 1997. "The Masking of History: Popular Images of the Nation on a Dominican Sugar Plantation." *New West Indian Guide* 71(3–4):227–48.

Martínez-Fernández, Luis. 1993. "Caudillos, Annexationism, and the Rivalry between Empires in the Dominican Republic, 1844–1874." *Diplomatic History* 17(4):571–97.

———. 1994. *Torn between Empires: Economy, Society, and Patterns of Political Thought in the Hispanic Caribbean.* Athens, Ga.: University of Georgia Press.

Mateo, Andrés L. 1993. *Mito y cultura en la Era de Trujillo.* Santo Domingo: Librería La Trinitaria.

McConahay, John B., and Joseph C. Hough, Jr. 1976. "Symbolic Racism." *Journal of Social Issues* 32(2):23–45.

Mejía Ricart, Tirso. 1985. "Haití en la formación de la nacionalidad dominicana." *Eme-Eme Estudios Dominicanos* 14(79):61–75.

Montaner, Carlos Alberto. 1983. *Fidel Castro y la Revolución Cubana.* Madrid: Editorial Playor.

Monte y Tejada, Antonio del. [1853] 1953. *Historia de Santo Domingo.* 3rd ed. 3 vols. Ciudad Trujillo: Impresora Dominicana.

Moreau de Saint-Méry, Méderic Louis Elie. [1796] 1944. *Descripción de la parte española de Santo Domingo.* Trans. Lic. C. Armando Rodríguez. Ciudad Trujillo: Editora Montalvo.

Moscoso Puello, Francisco Eugenio. [1913, 1930–35] 1974. *Cartas a Evelina.* Reprint. Santo Domingo: Editora Cosmos.

Moya Pons, Frank. 1977. *Historia colonial de Santo Domingo.* 3rd ed. Santiago: Universidad Católica Madre y Maestra.

———. 1986a. *El batey: Estudio socioeconómico de los bateyes del Consejo Estatal del Azúcar.* Santo Domingo: Fondo para el Avance de las Ciencias Sociales.

———. 1986b. *El pasado dominicano.* Santo Domingo: Fundación J. A. Caro Álvarez.

Murphy, Martin F. 1991. *Dominican Sugar Plantations: Production and Foreign Labor Integration.* New York: Praeger.

Nolasco, Sócrates. 1955. *Comentarios a la historia de Jean Price-Mars.* Ciudad Trujillo: Impresora Dominicana.

Núñez, Manuel. 1990. *El ocaso de la nación dominicana.* Santo Domingo: Alfa y Omega.

Núñez, Miguel Angel. 1996. "Peña Gómez opta por buscar sucesor en PRD." *Hoy,* 5 July, 1, 6.

ONAPLAN. 1981. *Participación de la mano de obra haitiana en el mercado laboral: Los casos de la caña y el café.* Santo Domingo: Secretariado Técnico de la Presidencia, Oficina Nacional de Planificación.

Orum, Anthony M. 1983. *Introduction to Political Sociology: The Social Anatomy of the Body Politic.* 2nd ed. Englewood Cliffs, N.J.: Prentice-Hall.

Ott, Thomas O. 1973. *The Haitian Revolution, 1789–1804.* Knoxville, Tenn.: University of Tennessee Press.

Oviedo, José. 1986. "La tradición autoritaria." Instituto Tecnológico de Santo Domingo. Typescript.

Para la historia dos cartas. 1943. Santiago: Editorial El Diario.

Peabody, Robert L., Susan Webb Hammond, Jean Torcom, Lynne P. Brown, Carolyn Thompson, and Robin Kolodny. 1990. "Interviewing Political Elites." *PS: Political Science and Politics* 23(3):451–55.

Peña Batlle, Manuel A. 1951. *La isla de La Tortuga.* Madrid: Ediciones Cultura Hispánica.

———. 1952. *El Tratado de Basilea y la desnacionalización del Santo Domingo español.* Ciudad Trujillo: Impresora Dominicana.

———. 1954a. *Orígenes del estado haitiano.* Ciudad Trujillo: Editora Montalvo.

———. 1954b. *Política de Trujillo.* Ciudad Trujillo: Impresora Dominicana.

———. [1946] 1988. *Historia de la cuestión fronteriza domínico-haitiana.* Reprint. Santo Domingo: Sociedad Dominicana de Bibliófilos.

Penn, Mark J. 1986. "Las elecciones dominicanas." *Listín Diario,* 11 June, 8.

Peñolguín, Santiago. 1940. *Vodú.* La Vega: Tip. La Palabra.

Penson, José F. 1959. *El Partido Dominicano.* Ciudad Trujillo: Editora del Caribe.

Pérez, José Joaquín. 1877. *Fantasías indígenas.* Santo Domingo: Imprenta de García Hermanos.

Pérez, Luis Julián. 1990. *Santo Domingo frente al destino.* 2nd ed. Santo Domingo: Taller.

Pérez, Máximo M. 1993. "El gobierno autoriza la venta alimentos, combustibles Haití." *Listín Diario,* 12 April, 1, 16.

Pérez Cabral, Pedro A. 1967. *La comunidad mulata: El caso socio-político de la República Dominicana.* Caracas: Gráfica Americana.

Pérez Memén, Fernando. 1987. *Estudios de historia de las ideas en Santo Domingo y en América.* Santo Domingo: Editorial Tiempo.

Perlmutter, Amos. 1981. *Modern Authoritarianism: A Comparative Institutional Analysis.* New Haven, Conn.: Yale University Press.

Pichardo, Bernardo. 1966. *Resumen de historia patria.* 5th ed. Santo Domingo: Editorial Librería Dominicana.

Pierre-Charles, Gérard. 1974. "Génesis de las naciones haitiana y dominicana." In *Política y sociología en Haití y la República Dominicana,* ed. Gérard Pierre-Charles. Mexico: UNAM.

Plant, Roger. 1987. *Sugar and Modern Slavery: A Tale of Two Countries.* London: Zed Books.

Plummer, Brenda Gayle. 1992. *Haiti and the United States: The Psychological Moment.* Athens, Ga.: University of Georgia Press.

Price-Mars, Jean. 1953. *La République d'Haïti et la République Dominicaine.* 2 vols. Port-au-Prince: Collection du Tricinquantenaire de l'Independance d'Haïti.

———. [1953] 1958. *La República de Haití y la República Dominicana.* 3 vols. Madrid: Colección del Tercer Cincuentenario de la Independencia de Haití.

Puig, Max. 1992. "Historia y política." In *Ayiti-República Dominicana: En el umbral de los años 90,* ed. CIPROS. Santo Domingo: CIPROS.

República Dominicana, Asamblea Nacional. 1994. *Constitución de la República Dominicana.* Santo Domingo: Editora El Estudiante.

Roberts, Peter. 1997. "The (Re)Construction of the Concept of 'Indio' in the National Identities of Cuba, the Dominican Republic and Puerto Rico." In *Caribe 2000: Definiciones, identidades y culturas regionales y/o nacionales,* ed. Lowell Fiet. San Juan: First Book Publishing.

Rodríguez de León, Francisco. 1996. *Balaguer y Trujillo: Entre la espada y la palabra.* Santo Domingo: Artes y Ediciones Caribe.

Rodríguez Demorizi, Emilio. 1946. *Documentos para la historia de la República Dominicana.* Vol. 2. Santiago: Editorial El Diario.

———. 1955a. *Invasiones haitianas de 1801, 1805 y 1822.* Ciudad Trujillo: Editora del Caribe.

———. 1955b. *La Era de Francia en Santo Domingo.* Ciudad Trujillo: Editora del Caribe.

———. 1957. *Guerra domínico-haitiana: Documentos para su estudio.* Ciudad Trujillo: Impresora Dominicana.

———. 1958. *Cesión de Santo Domingo a Francia.* Ciudad Trujillo: Impresora Dominicana.

———. 1959. *Documentos para la historia de la República Dominicana.* Vol. 3. Ciudad Trujillo: Impresora Dominicana.

———. 1971. *Música y baile en Santo Domingo.* Santo Domingo: Librería Hispaniola.

———. 1975. *Lengua y folklore de Santo Domingo.* Santiago: UCMM.

Rogoziński, Jan. 1994. *A Brief History of the Caribbean: From the Arawak and the Carib to the Present.* New York: Meridian.

Román, Miguel Alberto. 1949. *Compay Chano.* Ciudad Trujillo: Editorial del Caribe.

Rosario, Esteban. 1992. *Los dueños de la República Dominicana.* 2nd ed. Santo Domingo: Servicios Gráficos Oriental.

Rosario Adames, Fausto. 1994. "Los políticos en el diván." *Rumbo* 1(12):8–12.

Rosario Pérez, Angel S. del. 1957. *La exterminación añorada.* Ciudad Trujillo: n.p.

Sáez, José Luis. 1988. "Catolicismo e hispanidad en la oratoria de Trujillo." *Estudios Sociales* 21(73):89–104.

Sagás, Ernesto. 1988. "Politics and Praetorianism in the Dominican Republic: From Trujillo to Balaguer." Masters thesis. University of Florida.

———. 1993. "Antihaitianismo in the Dominican Republic." Ph.D. diss. University of Florida.

———. 1997. "The 1996 Presidential Elections in the Dominican Republic." *Electoral Studies* 16(1):103–7.

San Miguel, Pedro L. 1992. "Discurso racial e identidad nacional en la República Dominicana." *Op. Cit.* 7:67–120.

Sánchez y Sánchez, Carlos Augusto. 1958. *El caso domínico-haitiano (Separata).* Ciudad Trujillo: Editora Montalvo.

Sang Ben, Mu-Kien Adriana. 1991. *Buenaventura Báez: El caudillo del Sur (1844–1878).* Santo Domingo: Taller.

Sanz Lajara, José M. 1949. *Caonex.* Buenos Aires: Editorial Américalee.

Sarita, Esteban. 1993. "Majluta considera Aristide provocará discordia con RD." *Listín Diario,* 22 February, 4.

Sears, David O., Carl P. Hensler, and Leslie K. Speer. 1979. "Whites' Opposition to 'Busing': Self-Interest or Symbolic Politics?" *American Political Science Review* 73: 369–84.

Skidmore, Thomas E. 1993. *Black into White: Race and Nationality in Brazilian Thought.* 2nd ed. Durham, N.C.: Duke University Press.

Sommer, Doris. 1983. *One Master for Another: Populism as Patriarchal Rhetoric in Dominican Novels.* Lanham, Md.: University Press of America.

———. 1991. *Foundational Fictions: The National Romances of Latin America.* Berkeley, Calif.: University of California Press.

Tejada, Adriano Miguel. 1978. "El folklore como mecanismo de control político en Heureaux y Trujillo." *Eme-Eme Estudios Dominicanos* 6(34):19–39.

Tolentino Dipp, Hugo. 1973. "El fenómeno racial en Haití y en la República Dominicana." In *Problemas domínico-haitianos y del Caribe,* ed. Gérard Pierre-Charles. Mexico: UNAM.

———. 1992. *Raza e historia en Santo Domingo: Los orígenes del prejuicio racial en América.* 2nd ed. Santo Domingo: Fundación Cultural Dominicana.

Tomasek, Robert D. 1968. "The Haitian-Dominican Republic Controversy of 1963 and the Organization of American States." *Orbis* 12:294–313.

Torres-Saillant, Silvio. 1998. "The Tribulations of Blackness: Stages in Dominican Racial Identity." *Latin American Perspectives* 25(3):126–46.

Trujillo, Rafael L. 1955. *Evolución de la democracia en Santo Domingo.* San Cristóbal: Dirección General de Estadística.

Utrera, Fray Cipriano de. 1978. *Noticias históricas de Santo Domingo.* 5 vols. Ed. Emilio Rodríguez Demorizi. Santo Domingo: Taller.

Vallejo, Rubén Darío. 1993. "¿Mito o realidad?: La venganza de la haitiana." *Listín Diario,* 6 June, 5-D.

Van Dijk, Teun A. 1987. *Communicating Racism: Ethnic Prejudice in Thought and Talk.* Newbury Park, Calif.: Sage Publications.

———. 1993. *Elite Discourse and Racism.* Newbury Park, Calif.: Sage Publications.

Vargas-Lundius, Rosemary. 1991. *Peasants in Distress: Poverty and Unemployment in the Dominican Republic.* Boulder, Colo.: Westview Press.

Vásquez, Rafael (general undersecretary and coordinator of the P.R.D. in the United States). 1994. Interview by author. Tape recording. New York, N.Y., 12 December.

Vega, Bernardo. 1988. *Trujillo y Haití.* Vol. 1, 1930–37. Santo Domingo: Fundación Cultural Dominicana.

———. 1991. *En la década perdida: Ponencias, conferencias y artículos, 1984–1990.* Santo Domingo: Fundación Cultural Dominicana.

———. 1993a. *Kennedy y Bosch: Aportes al estudio de las relaciones internacionales del gobierno constitucional de 1963.* Santo Domingo: Fundación Cultural Dominicana.

———. 1993b. "¿Qué hacer con el CEA?" *Listín Diario,* 10 March, 6.

———. 1994a. "El antihaitianismo dominicano y sus etapas." *Listín Diario,* 15 June, 6.

———. 1994b. "Las encuestas y nuestras elecciones." *Listín Diario,* 12 May, 7.

———. 1995. *Trujillo y Haití.* Vol. 2, 1937–38. Santo Domingo: Fundación Cultural Dominicana.

Velázquez Mainardi, Miguel A. 1991. "La nueva provocación de Aristide." *El Nacional,* 29 September.

Veloz Maggiolo, Marcio. 1996. "La acusación de 'negrofilia': Un recurso temprano de la política racista dominicana." *Ecos* 4(5):209–16.

Veras, Ramón Antonio. 1983. *Inmigración, haitianos, esclavitud.* Santo Domingo: Taller.

Viau, Alfred. 1955. *Negros, mulatos, blancos o sangre, nada más que sangre.* Ciudad Trujillo: Impresora Montalvo.

Welles, Sumner. 1986. *La viña de Naboth: La República Dominicana, 1844–1924.* 5th ed. 2 vols. Trans. Manfredo A. Moore. Santo Domingo: Taller.

Wells, Henry. 1985. "Puerto Rico: The Question of Statehood, Commonwealth, or Nation." In *Latin American Politics and Development,* ed. Howard J. Wiarda and Harvey F. Kline. Boulder, Colo.: Westview Press.

Wiarda, Howard J. 1968. *Dictatorship and Development: The Methods of Control in Trujillo's Dominican Republic.* Gainesville, Fla.: University of Florida Press.

Wiarda, Howard J., and Michael J. Kryzanek. 1992. *The Dominican Republic: A Caribbean Crucible.* 2nd ed. Boulder, Colo.: Westview Press.

Wilentz, Amy. 1989. *The Rainy Season: Haiti since Duvalier.* New York: Simon and Schuster.

Wilhelms, Saskia K. S. 1994. *Haitian and Dominican Sugarcane Workers in Dominican Bateyes: Patterns and Effects of Prejudice, Stereotypes, and Discrimination.* Hamburg, Germany: Lit.

Williams, Eric. 1984. *From Columbus to Castro: The History of the Caribbean, 1492–1969.* New York: Vintage Books.

Zaglul, Jesús M. 1992. "Una identificación nacional 'defensiva': El antihaitianismo nacionalista de Joaquín Balaguer—Una lectura de 'La isla al revés'." *Estudios Sociales* 25(87):29–65.

Ernesto Sagás teaches in the Department of Puerto Rican and Hispanic Caribbean Studies of Rutgers, the State University of New Jersey. He has published articles on Dominican politics and migration.

INDEX